A Gift For

_____

From

_____

STRENGTH *for the* SOUL *from* OUR DAILY BREAD

Cherish

Quiet Moments *for* Moms and Dads

Discovery House Publishers

Books, music, and videos that feed the soul with the Word of God

Box 3566 Grand Rapids, MI 49501

Discovery House Publishers is affiliated with RBC Ministries,
Grand Rapids, Michigan.

Discovery House books are distributed to the trade exclusively by
Barbour Publishing Inc., Uhrichsville, Ohio.

Requests for permission to quote from this book should be directed
to Permissions Department, Discovery House Publishers,
P.O. Box 3566, Grand Rapids, MI 49501.

All Scripture quotations, unless otherwise indicated, are taken
from the *New International Version*® NIV.® Copyright © 1973, 1978,
1984 by International Bible Society. Used by permission of Zondervan.
All rights reserved.

Scripture quotations followed by NKJV are taken from the
New King James Version, © 1982 by Thomas Nelson, Inc.
Used by permission. All rights reserved.

Interior design by Sherri L. Hoffman

Printed in the United States of America
08 09 10 11 12 / CHG / 10 9 8 7 6 5 4 3 2

Introduction

Since April 1956, millions of readers around the world have found daily inspiration, hope, comfort, and biblical truth from the pages of *Our Daily Bread*. Now you can find encouragement and quiet moments of inspiration from one of the most beloved devotionals, compiled into one convenient volume.

We believe that this book will be of help to you and those you know in every circumstance of life. May it and the Word of God bring strength to your soul.

Other books in the Strength for the Soul
from *Our Daily Bread* series

Christmas
Comfort
Grief
Hope
Peace
Prayer
Trust

Seasons of Motherhood

Now there was a man in Jerusalem called Simeon, who was righteous and devout. He was waiting for the consolation of Israel, and the Holy Spirit was upon him. It had been revealed to him by the Holy Spirit that he would not die before he had seen the Lord's Christ. Moved by the Spirit, he went into the temple courts. When the parents brought in the child Jesus to do for him what the custom of the Law required, Simeon took him in his arms and praised God, saying:

> "Sovereign Lord, as you have promised,
>   you now dismiss your servant in peace.
> For my eyes have seen your salvation,
>   which you have prepared in the sight of all people,
> a light for revelation to the Gentiles
>   and for glory to your people Israel."

The child's father and mother marveled at what was said about him. Then Simeon blessed them and said to Mary, his mother: "This child is destined to cause the falling and rising of many in Israel, and to be a sign that will be spoken against, so that the thoughts of many hearts will be revealed. And a sword will pierce your own soul too."

—LUKE 2:25–35

As a pastor, I've ministered to many women during their seasons of motherhood. I have called on mothers in the hospital and rejoiced with them for their precious baby who had come into the world. I've counseled with anxious mothers and tried to assure them that God was watching over their rebellious teenager. I've stood with mothers at the bedside of an injured or ill child and felt their pain. And I've cried with them in their grief when their son or daughter died.

Mary, the mother of Jesus, also experienced these times of joy and sorrow. What joy when the Christ-child was born! (Luke 2:7). What excitement when the shepherds and later the wise men came to worship Him! (vv. 8–20; Matthew 2:1–12). What uneasiness when Simeon prophesied that a sword would pierce her soul! (Luke 2:35). And what heart-wrenching grief as Mary watched her Son dying on the cross! (John 19:25–30). But her seasons of motherhood didn't end with that terrible scene. She rejoiced that He rose from the grave. And because she trusted Him as her Savior, she is now in heaven with Him.

A mother experiences great joys and intense sorrows. But if she submits her life to God, every season of her motherhood serves His eternal purposes. —HERB VANDER LUGT

Learning from Leandra

"I am the true vine, and my Father is the gardener. He cuts off every branch in me that bears no fruit, while every branch that does bear fruit he prunes so that it will be even more fruitful. You are already clean because of the word I have spoken to you. Remain in me, and I will remain in you. No branch can bear fruit by itself; it must remain in the vine. Neither can you bear fruit unless you remain in me.

"I am the vine; you are the branches. If a man remains in me and I in him, he will bear much fruit; apart from me you can do nothing. If anyone does not remain in me, he is like a branch that is thrown away and withers; such branches are picked up, thrown into the fire and burned. If you remain in me and my words remain in you, ask whatever you wish, and it will be given you. This is to my Father's glory, that you bear much fruit, showing yourselves to be my disciples."

—JOHN 15:1–8

Leandra is three years old. She has bright brown eyes and a very good mind. One day I was babysitting her, and she was watching her brother Max play games on my computer. Suddenly she announced that she was going to get a snack. "I do it myself!" she said emphatically.

"I'll help you," I said, and began to follow her. She repeated firmly, "I do it myself!" I watched her walk down the stairs. She turned, saw me, and said, "You stay upstairs, Grandpa. Keep an eye on Max." I tried not to laugh. At the bottom of the stairs she turned back, put one hand on her hip, and said, "I mean it, Grandpa!" I backed out of sight and roared with laughter. Later I checked on her. She had opened the refrigerator, found some pudding, and gotten a spoon, but she needed me to open the container for her.

I thought later that there's a lot of that spirit of independence in me. I too want to "do it myself" when it comes to growing and serving as a believer in Jesus Christ. Yet I need to realize that even though I may think I don't need His help, I really do. Without it, I am unable to produce the kind of spiritual fruit Jesus talked about in John 15.

We must remember the words of our Lord, who said, "Apart from me you can do nothing" (John 15:5).—DAVE EGNER

Created in God's Image

And God said, "Let the land produce living creatures according to their kinds: livestock, creatures that move along the ground, and wild animals, each according to its kind." And it was so. God made the wild animals according to their kinds, the livestock according to their kinds, and all the creatures that move along the ground according to their kinds. And God saw that it was good.

Then God said, "Let us make man in our image, in our likeness, and let them rule over the fish of the sea and the birds of the air, over the livestock, over all the earth, and over all the creatures that move along the ground."

So God created man in his own image,
 in the image of God he created him;
 male and female he created them . . .

God saw all that he had made, and it was very good. And there was evening, and there was morning—the sixth day.

—GENESIS 1:24–27, 31

The colorful folder I received through the mail advertised a series of books describing "the most fascinating study of man's origin ever published." The slick advertisement suggests that through eons of time primitive matter evolved into living creatures that eventually became modern man. From this pseudoscientific presentation I can only conclude that my existence is the result of a chemical accident, and that my life has no real purpose. I am a pathetic animal indeed!

The Bible declares that man was brought into being by a special act of the Creator Himself, who breathed into him "the breath of life" (Genesis 2:7). He was made in the image of God that he might live for Him and enjoy Him forever.

If we believe we are the products of chance, however, without meaning or destiny, our behavior will merely reflect a concern for "the next banana." But because we are made in the likeness of God, our lives have significance. We are to manifest in thought, word, and deed the eternal glory and purpose of our Designer—the One who revealed Himself in Jesus Christ!

Recognizing that you are created in God's image and are not just an animal, how will you live today?

—MART DE HAAN

Parents' Ten Commands

Blessed are all who fear the LORD,
   who walk in his ways.
You will eat the fruit of your labor;
   blessings and prosperity will be yours.
Your wife will be like a fruitful vine
   within your house;
   your sons will be like olive shoots
   around your table.
Thus is the man blessed
   who fears the LORD.
May the LORD bless you from Zion
   all the days of your life;
   may you see the prosperity of Jerusalem,
and may you live to see your children's children.
   Peace be upon Israel.

—PSALM 128

Children come without guarantees. No matter how well we take care of them, they don't always perform as we think they should. They're hard to steer. Or they may lose their "brakes."

But this doesn't mean we as parents are without responsibility. We must help our children grow into godly people. Author David Wilkerson said, "Good parents do not always produce good children, but devoted, dedicated, hardworking mothers and fathers can weigh the balance in favor of decency and moral character."

To assist in your quest to be good parents, here are 10 commandments for guiding children.

1. Teach them, using God's Word (Deuteronomy 6:4–9).
2. Tell them what's right and wrong (1 Kings 1:6).
3. See them as gifts from God (Psalm 127:3).
4. Guide them in godly ways (Proverbs 22:6).
5. Discipline them (Proverbs 29:17).
6. Love them unconditionally (Luke 15:11–32).
7. Do not provoke them to wrath (Ephesians 6:4).
8. Earn their respect by example (1 Timothy 3:4).
9. Provide for their physical needs (1 Timothy 5:8).
10. Pass your faith along to them (2 Timothy 1:5).

There are no guarantees. But we can have an edge in trying to "weigh the balance." —DAVE BRANON

Grow, Baby!

Therefore, rid yourselves of all malice and all deceit, hypocrisy, envy, and slander of every kind. Like newborn babies, crave pure spiritual milk, so that by it you may grow up in your salvation, now that you have tasted that the Lord is good.

As you come to him, the living Stone—rejected by men but chosen by God and precious to him—you also, like living stones, are being built into a spiritual house to be a holy priesthood, offering spiritual sacrifices acceptable to God through Jesus Christ . . .

But you are a chosen people, a royal priesthood, a holy nation, a people belonging to God, that you may declare the praises of him who called you out of darkness into his wonderful light. Once you were not a people, but now you are the people of God; once you had not received mercy, but now you have received mercy.

—1 Peter 2:1–5, 9–10

Whenever children visit relatives, they often hear this kind of greeting: "My, haven't you grown!" This embarrasses them, but inside they're glad they've outgrown babyhood. Not that babyhood is bad. How else can life begin? But it is sad when babies remain babies.

Sometimes mature Christians, eager to keep new converts from stagnating in their growth, make them feel guilty for being babies and rush them down the road to maturity before they are ready.

In 1 Peter 2, the apostle affirmed that spiritual babyhood is normal. Instead of forcing newborns to run before they can walk, he encouraged them to crave the wholesome milk of Christ's basic teaching. He knew that as they continued to take in milk, in time they would move on to solid food and maturity (Hebrews 5:14). What a joy to see that happen!

Several years ago I received a phone call from a friend, a former drug addict and now a Christian. "Hi, Chris," I responded cheerily. "How are you doing?" A long, worrisome pause made me wonder, Had he slipped back? Then came words that uplifted my heart: "Growing, Joanie, growing!" That said it all.

I hope you can say the same.   —JOANIE YODER

Adam's Legacy

Therefore, just as sin entered the world through one man, and death through sin, and in this way death came to all men, because all sinned—for before the law was given, sin was in the world. But sin is not taken into account when there is no law. Nevertheless, death reigned from the time of Adam to the time of Moses, even over those who did not sin by breaking a command, as did Adam, who was a pattern of the one to come.

But the gift is not like the trespass. For if the many died by the trespass of the one man, how much more did God's grace and the gift that came by the grace of the one man, Jesus Christ, overflow to the many! Again, the gift of God is not like the result of the one man's sin: The judgment followed one sin and brought condemnation, but the gift followed many trespasses and brought justification. For if, by the trespass of the one man, death reigned through that one man, how much more will those who receive God's abundant provision of grace and of the gift of righteousness reign in life through the one man, Jesus Christ.

—ROMANS 5:12–17

*O*ur new grandson Jackson had fine features, soft blemish-free skin, and ten tiny fingers and toes on two little hands and feet. How could any proud Grampa not see him as a "perfect" baby? He certainly was a miracle of divine formation (Psalm 139:13–14).

The apostle Paul gave us a broader view of such "perfect" little infants when he wrote, "Just as sin entered the world through one man, and death through sin . . . Nevertheless death reigned from the time of Adam to the time of Moses, even over those who did not sin by breaking a command, as did Adam" (Romans 5:12–14). In other words, every child is born with a tendency to sin. But that's not Paul's final word. He also wrote about Jesus, the "last Adam," who became a "life-giving spirit" (1 Corinthians 15:45).

Long after man's first sin, a baby was born who was God incarnate (John 1:14). God made Christ, "who had no sin to be sin for us" (2 Corinthians 5:21). When we trust Jesus as our Savior, the Holy Spirit creates within us a new desire to do what is pleasing to God. The flesh still has its pull, but the pull of the Spirit is stronger.

In the "first Adam" we're all sinners. But let's concentrate on who we are in the "last Adam."　　　—DENNIS DE HAAN

Greatly Valued

David asked, "Is there anyone still left of the house of Saul to whom I can show kindness for Jonathan's sake?"

Now there was a servant of Saul's household named Ziba. They called him to appear before David, and the king said to him, "Are you Ziba?"

"Your servant," he replied.

The king asked, "Is there no one still left of the house of Saul to whom I can show God's kindness?"

Ziba answered the king, "There is still a son of Jonathan; he is crippled in both feet."

"Where is he?" the king asked.

Ziba answered, "He is at the house of Makir son of Ammiel in Lo Debar."

So King David had him brought from Lo Debar, from the house of Makir son of Ammiel. When Mephibosheth son of Jonathan, the son of Saul, came to David, he bowed down to pay him honor. David said, "Mephibosheth!"

"Your servant," he replied.

"Don't be afraid," David said to him, "for I will surely show you kindness for the sake of your father Jonathan. I will restore to you all the land that belonged to your grandfather Saul, and you will always eat at my table." —2 SAMUEL 9:1–7

British factory worker and his wife were excited when, after many years of marriage, they discovered they were going to have their first child. According to author Jill Briscoe, who told this true story, the man eagerly relayed the good news to his fellow workers. He told them God had answered his prayers. But they made fun of him for asking God for a child.

When the baby was born, he was diagnosed as having Down's syndrome. As the father made his way to work for the first time after the birth, he wondered how to face his co-workers. "God, please give me wisdom," he prayed. Just as he feared, some said mockingly, "So, God gave you this child!" The new father stood for a long time, silently asking God for help. At last he said, "I'm glad the Lord gave this child to me and not to you."

As this man accepted his disabled son as God's gift to him, so David was pleased to show kindness to Saul's grandson who was "crippled in both feet" (2 Samuel 9:3). Some may have rejected Mephibosheth because he was lame, but David's action showed that he valued him greatly.

In God's eyes, every person is important. He sent His only Son to die for us. May we remember with gratitude how much He values each human life. —DAVE BRANON

19

God's Work of Art

But now you must rid yourselves of all such things as these: anger, rage, malice, slander, and filthy language from your lips. Do not lie to each other, since you have taken off your old self with its practices and have put on the new self, which is being renewed in knowledge in the image of its Creator. Here there is no Greek or Jew, circumcised or uncircumcised, barbarian, Scythian, slave or free, but Christ is all, and is in all.

Therefore, as God's chosen people, holy and dearly loved, clothe yourselves with compassion, kindness, humility, gentleness and patience. Bear with each other and forgive whatever grievances you may have against one another. Forgive as the Lord forgave you. And over all these virtues put on love, which binds them all together in perfect unity.

Let the peace of Christ rule in your hearts, since as members of one body you were called to peace. And be thankful. Let the word of Christ dwell in you richly as you teach and admonish one another with all wisdom, and as you sing psalms, hymns and spiritual songs with gratitude in your hearts to God. And whatever you do, whether in word or deed, do it all in the name of the Lord Jesus, giving thanks to God the Father through him.

—COLOSSIANS 3:8–17

*V*incent Van Gogh bought a mirror and used his own likeness in many of his paintings. Rembrandt also used himself as a model, completing nearly one hundred self-portraits. These artists had a good example, that of God Himself, who used His own likeness as the pattern for His crown jewel of creation (Genesis 1:27).

Henry Ward Beecher, the famous nineteenth-century clergyman, said, "Every artist dips his brush in his own soul, and paints his own nature into his pictures." In everything we create—works of art, music, literature, even our children—a bit of ourselves is revealed. The same is true of God; each of us reveals a bit of Him. The image may be tarnished, but it's always there and is never beyond repair.

Superficial changes won't fix what's wrong with us, however. Clothes, cosmetics, and surgical procedures can make us look like everyone else, not like the unique masterpiece God designed each of us to be. We need a whole new "self" (Colossians 3:10), one that is renewed in His image and dressed in the wardrobe of compassion, kindness, humility, gentleness, and patience (v. 12).

To improve your "self" image, put on the character of God and display His image in all its glory.

—JULIE ACKERMAN LINK

Meeting Jesus

"Do not let your hearts be troubled. Trust in God; trust also in me. In my Father's house are many rooms; if it were not so, I would have told you. I am going there to prepare a place for you. And if I go and prepare a place for you, I will come back and take you to be with me that you also may be where I am. You know the way to the place where I am going."

Thomas said to him, "Lord, we don't know where you are going, so how can we know the way?"

Jesus answered, "I am the way and the truth and the life. No one comes to the Father except through me. If you really knew me, you would know my Father as well. From now on, you do know him and have seen him."

Philip said, "Lord, show us the Father and that will be enough for us."

Jesus answered: "Don't you know me, Philip, even after I have been among you such a long time? Anyone who has seen me has seen the Father. How can you say, 'Show us the Father'? Don't you believe that I am in the Father, and that the Father is in me? The words I say to you are not just my own. Rather, it is the Father, living in me, who is doing his work. Believe me when I say that I am in the Father and the Father is in me; or at least believe on the evidence of the miracles themselves. —JOHN 14:1–11

*D*o you believe in God? When George Gallup and his associates put that question to a cross section of Americans, the vast majority responded yes. When asked what they thought about God, 84% saw Him as a heavenly Father who can be reached by prayer, 5% viewed Him as an idea but not as a being, 5% said they didn't believe in Him, 2% said He is an impersonal creator, and 4% said they didn't know.

Most people, then, believe in a Supreme Being. They also believe that the God who created the universe cares enough for insignificant human beings to listen as they tell Him about their needs and desires. But beyond those rather vague notions, there is little understanding of who God is.

Philip's plea, "Lord, show us the Father and that will be enough for us" (John 14:8), is still the silent cry of countless hearts. He was asking Jesus to reveal what God is really like. Jesus replied, "Anyone who has seen me has seen the Father" (v. 9). The invisible God has been made visible in Jesus (Hebrews 1:3). As we observe His life in the pages of Scripture, we see the very heart and holiness of God the Father.

You may believe in God, but you can also know Him personally by meeting His Son Jesus. —VERNON GROUNDS

Set in Concrete

A good name is more desirable than great riches;
    to be esteemed is better than silver or gold.
Rich and poor have this in common:
    The LORD is the Maker of them all.
A prudent man sees danger and takes refuge,
    but the simple keep going and suffer for it.
Humility and the fear of the LORD
    bring wealth and honor and life.
In the paths of the wicked lie thorns and snares,
    but he who guards his soul stays far from them.
Train a child in the way he should go,
    and when he is old he will not turn from it.

—PROVERBS 22:1–6

A young mother in Kansas made an unusual request of a workman who was smoothing out the freshly poured concrete of a new sidewalk. She asked if she could press her baby's feet onto the concrete. When the man said yes, she stood the child on the wet cement and pointed his toes in the direction of a nearby church. Although we don't know what prompted that mother to do this, she apparently wanted to make a permanent impression that would influence the future direction of her little boy's life.

This unusual expression of concern and commitment should reflect the desire of all Christian parents for the spiritual welfare of their children. We must position our young ones on the right way and recognize the importance of the church in their lives. Our children's spiritual training must begin at an early age. We have the responsibility to encourage them to receive the Lord Jesus Christ as their Savior as soon as they are old enough to understand the meaning of salvation. If we do that, we will cultivate in them a respect for the church and instill in their hearts a love for God and His Word.

By our teaching, our example, and our prayers, let's set our children's feet in the right direction. —RICHARD DE HAAN

We Know

Peter asked, "Lord, are you telling this parable to us, or to everyone?"

The Lord answered, "Who then is the faithful and wise manager, whom the master puts in charge of his servants to give them their food allowance at the proper time? It will be good for that servant whom the master finds doing so when he returns. I tell you the truth, he will put him in charge of all his possessions. But suppose the servant says to himself, 'My master is taking a long time in coming,' and he then begins to beat the menservants and maidservants and to eat and drink and get drunk. The master of that servant will come on a day when he does not expect him and at an hour he is not aware of. He will cut him to pieces and assign him a place with the unbelievers.

"That servant who knows his master's will and does not get ready or does not do what his master wants will be beaten with many blows. But the one who does not know and does things deserving punishment will be beaten with few blows. From everyone who has been given much, much will be demanded; and from the one who has been entrusted with much, much more will be asked."

—LUKE 12:41–48

My son Steve knows his "floppy hat" is reserved for life's most informal times. This hat, which would look good on a fisherman by the lake, is not to be worn to church or school. So, when he grabbed it one morning on his way out of the house to catch the school bus, he knew he was breaking a rule.

Parents understand these kinds of battles. We recognize that our children will test our rules, and we are not surprised when they challenge us. They know they aren't supposed to watch certain TV programs or stay out too late or use a disrespectful tone of voice or fight with a sibling. Yet they still do.

This is not unlike the attitude we sometimes take with our heavenly Father. We know what is right and wrong (James 4:17). We've read the Bible. We've sensed in our hearts the conviction of the Holy Spirit. We know. Yet we test God.

We know it's wrong to speak disparagingly of others. We know it's not right to neglect those in need. We know we should witness to our neighbor. We know we should pray. We know that when the Lord returns we should be faithfully serving and obeying Him (Luke 12:42–43). We know!

How it pleases God when we act on what we already know!
—DAVE BRANON

Good Dads

Consider him who endured such opposition from sinful men, so that you will not grow weary and lose heart.

In your struggle against sin, you have not yet resisted to the point of shedding your blood. And you have forgotten that word of encouragement that addresses you as sons:

> "My son, do not make light of the Lord's discipline,
>   and do not lose heart when he rebukes you,
> because the Lord disciplines those he loves,
>   and he punishes everyone he accepts as a son."

Endure hardship as discipline; God is treating you as sons. For what son is not disciplined by his father? If you are not disciplined (and everyone undergoes discipline), then you are illegitimate children and not true sons. Moreover, we have all had human fathers who disciplined us and we respected them for it. How much more should we submit to the Father of our spirits and live! Our fathers disciplined us for a little while as they thought best; but God disciplines us for our good, that we may share in his holiness. No discipline seems pleasant at the time, but painful. Later on, however, it produces a harvest of righteousness and peace for those who have been trained by it.

—HEBREWS 12:3–11

Columnist Leonard Pitts Jr. grew up with a father he describes as physically present but emotionally absent. In his first book on parenting, Pitts openly chronicles his struggle to come to terms with his alcoholic father and the climate of fear he had created in their home. Pitts challenges all men to resolve the resentment toward their absent or abusive fathers instead of passing it on to the next generation.

There's a passage in Hebrews 12 that applies to all Christians, but it has special relevance to dads. It reads: "Make every effort to live in peace with all men and to be holy; without holiness no one will see the Lord. See to it that no one misses the grace of God and that no bitter root grows up to cause trouble and defile many" (vv. 14–15).

Think of what could happen in our families if we emptied our hearts of bitterness and made peaceful relationships our goal! If we have been blessed with a wise and loving father, we should be grateful and follow his example. But if our father has failed us, we must rely on God's grace, resolve our anger toward him, and strive to be the kind of dad we never had. It won't be easy, but with our heavenly Father as a perfect example, we can learn to be good dads. —DAVID McCASLAND

Parents Who Pray

Then little children were brought to Jesus for him to place his hands on them and pray for them. But the disciples rebuked those who brought them.

Jesus said, "Let the little children come to me, and do not hinder them, for the kingdom of heaven belongs to such as these." When he had placed his hands on them, he went on from there.

—MATTHEW 19:13–15

A young mother sent these lines to a magazine: "I wish I could wrap my children in bubble wrap to protect them from the big, bad world outside."

Author Stormie Omartian understands how that mother feels. In her book *The Power of a Praying Parent*, she writes, "One day I cried out to God, saying, 'Lord, this is too much for me. I can't keep a twenty-four-hours-a-day, moment-by-moment watch on my son. How can I ever have peace?' "

God responded by leading Stormie and her husband to become praying parents. They began to intercede for their son daily, mentioning the details of his life in prayer.

The desire to wrap our children in bubble wrap to protect them is rooted in fear, a common tendency, especially among mothers. Wrapping them in prayer, as Jesus did (Matthew 19:13–15), is a powerful alternative. He cares more about our children than we do, so we can release them into His hands by praying for them. He doesn't promise us that nothing bad will happen to them. But as we pray, He will give us the peace we long for (Philippians 4:6–7).

This challenge is for all parents—even those whose children have grown up: Don't ever stop wrapping your children in prayer!

—JOANIE YODER

It's Sally!

Children, obey your parents in the Lord, for this is right. "Honor your father and mother"—which is the first commandment with a promise—"that it may go well with you and that you may enjoy long life on the earth."

Fathers, do not exasperate your children; instead, bring them up in the training and instruction of the Lord.

—EPHESIANS 6:1–4

*B*enjamin West was just trying to be a good babysitter for his little sister Sally. While his mother was out, Benjamin found some bottles of colored ink and proceeded to paint Sally's portrait. But by the time Mrs. West returned, ink blots stained the table, chairs, and floor. Benjamin's mother surveyed the mess without a word until she saw the picture. Picking it up she exclaimed, "Why, it's Sally!" And she bent down and kissed her young son.

In 1763, when he was twenty-five years old, Benjamin West was selected as history painter to England's King George III. He became one of the most celebrated artists of his day. Commenting on his start as an artist, he said, "My mother's kiss made me a painter." Her encouragement did far more than a rebuke ever could have done.

The apostle Paul instructed parents: "Do not exasperate your children; instead, bring them up in the training and instruction of the Lord" (Ephesians 6:4).

It's easy to notice the wrong in a child, but difficult to look beyond an innocent offense to see an act of creativity and love. What a challenge to raise our children according to God's standards, knowing when to say, "It's a mess!" and when to say, "Why, it's Sally!" —DAVID MCCASLAND

Fitness Training

Oh, how I love your law!
*   I meditate on it all day long.*
Your commands make me wiser than my enemies,
*   for they are ever with me.*
I have more insight than all my teachers,
*   for I meditate on your statutes.*
I have more understanding than the elders,
*   for I obey your precepts.*
I have kept my feet from every evil path
*   so that I might obey your word.*
I have not departed from your laws,
*   for you yourself have taught me.*
How sweet are your words to my taste,
*   sweeter than honey to my mouth!*
I gain understanding from your precepts;
*   therefore I hate every wrong path.*

*—*Psalm 119:97–104

My wife is an avid exerciser. She walks, rollerblades, and bikes to keep in shape. Because of her interest in exercise, she has encouraged our children to participate in sports activities at school and to exercise along with her.

Why does she feel this is so important? It's simple: When she doesn't exercise several times a week, she doesn't feel physically fit. She feels sluggish and lethargic. She feels that her heart is not being strengthened as it should be.

But she doesn't stop with the physical part of her life. She also participates in spiritual exercise. She knows that in our walk with God we need "heart exercise" to stay fit.

The writer of Psalm 119 saw the importance of daily spiritual exercise. He loved the Word of God, meditated on it throughout the day, and obeyed it. His prayers were from his whole heart, and his hope for each new day came directly from God's Word.

How much more spiritually healthy we would be if we engaged in a godly fitness training program that matched that of the psalmist! Do you read the Bible, meditate on its truths, and pray each day? If not, begin spiritual fitness training today.   —DAVE BRANON

Father's Touch

That which was from the beginning, which we have heard, which we have seen with our eyes, which we have looked at and our hands have touched—this we proclaim concerning the Word of life. The life appeared; we have seen it and testify to it, and we proclaim to you the eternal life, which was with the Father and has appeared to us. We proclaim to you what we have seen and heard, so that you also may have fellowship with us. And our fellowship is with the Father and with his Son, Jesus Christ. We write this to make our joy complete.

This is the message we have heard from him and declare to you: God is light; in him there is no darkness at all. If we claim to have fellowship with him yet walk in the darkness, we lie and do not live by the truth. But if we walk in the light, as he is in the light, we have fellowship with one another, and the blood of Jesus, his Son, purifies us from all sin. —1 JOHN 1:1–7

How things have changed since I became a father! When each of our four sons was born, I waited anxiously in the waiting room while my wife, Margaret, was in the delivery room.

But my sons who have families of their own attended a series of preparation classes and were with their wives when their babies were born. They shared together the excitement and joy of seeing a precious new life come into the world.

This is not for the benefit of the mother and father alone, however. Medical authorities now recognize that the infant needs to have visual and physical contact with both parents soon after it is born. Studies show that babies who are lovingly handled in the first twelve hours after birth smile more and cry less in their first few years than those who are denied the touch technique.

It is even more important for us to be in touch with our heavenly Father. God's children keep in conscious contact with Him by letting Him speak to them through the Bible, and by responding to Him in prayer.

Have you felt the Father's touch today? You need that quiet hour when you open His Word to yourself, and your heart to Him.   —RICHARD DE HAAN

"Not Know!"

In that day you will say:
  "I will praise you, O LORD.
Although you were angry with me,
    your anger has turned away
    and you have comforted me.
Surely God is my salvation;
    I will trust and not be afraid.
The LORD, the LORD, is my strength and my song;
    he has become my salvation."
With joy you will draw water
    from the wells of salvation.
In that day you will say:
  "Give thanks to the LORD, call on his name;
make known among the nations what he has done,
    and proclaim that his name is exalted.
Sing to the LORD, for he has done glorious things;
    let this be known to all the world.
Shout aloud and sing for joy, people of Zion,
    for great is the Holy One of Israel among you."

—ISAIAH 12

Two-year-old Max was securely buckled in his seat in Grandpa's pickup truck. He was waiting for Dad and Grandpa to stop talking so he could go for a ride. His mother poked her head in the truck and said, "Where are you going, Max?" "Not know," he replied, raising his little arms.

"What are you going to do?" she asked. "Not know," came the answer again.

"Well," she asked, "do you want to come back in the house with me?"

"No!" came the quick reply as he settled himself more firmly, waiting to begin his adventure.

"That little boy taught me a lesson I needed right then," his mother, Sheryl, told me later. She was soon to give birth to another baby, and she had reason to be unsure of what was ahead. "He didn't know where he was going or what he was going to do, but he trusted Grandpa completely. Max's confidence in Grandpa is the kind of trust I need in my heavenly Father."

If you are in one of those periods of life when you don't know what lies ahead, or you don't know what to do about some critical issue, it might help to think about it that way. God wants you to have the confidence in Him to say, "I will trust and not be afraid" (Isaiah 12:2). —DAVE EGNER

It's for Sure!

Now, brothers, about times and dates we do not need to write to you, for you know very well that the day of the Lord will come like a thief in the night. While people are saying, "Peace and safety," destruction will come on them suddenly, as labor pains on a pregnant woman, and they will not escape.

But you, brothers, are not in darkness so that this day should surprise you like a thief. You are all sons of the light and sons of the day. We do not belong to the night or to the darkness. So then, let us not be like others, who are asleep, but let us be alert and self-controlled. For those who sleep, sleep at night, and those who get drunk, get drunk at night. But since we belong to the day, let us be self-controlled, putting on faith and love as a breastplate, and the hope of salvation as a helmet. For God did not appoint us to suffer wrath but to receive salvation through our Lord Jesus Christ. He died for us so that, whether we are awake or asleep, we may live together with him. Therefore encourage one another and build each other up, just as in fact you are doing.

—1 Thessalonians 5:1–11

*B*efore our second child was born, my wife and I attended a childbirth class offered by the hospital. During the course we watched a film designed to relieve the fears of expectant parents. All of us had questions like: When will the labor begin? Will there be plenty of time to get to the hospital? Will the delivery be hard? And what about our baby? Will it be a boy or a girl? Will it be large or small? Will it be healthy?

The narrator then summed it up like this: "Yes, there are so many questions left unanswered. But one thing is for sure: You will deliver. You will give birth!" The class laughed. One thing was certain—the baby would come.

The experience reminded me of the Lord's second coming. We have so many questions about it. What will it be like? Will it be a startling experience? Will we be happy when we see Jesus? Where will we be when it occurs? Will we be living, or will we be among those who are raised from the dead?

Yes, as we anticipate the birth of that new day, there are many unanswered questions. But one thing is for sure—He is coming! That is why we should prepare ourselves through faith, hope, and love (1 Thessalonians 5:8). Then we will be ready for the blessed event. —MART DE HAAN

Changed!

The LORD spoke to Manasseh and his people, but they paid no attention. So the LORD brought against them the army commanders of the king of Assyria, who took Manasseh prisoner, put a hook in his nose, bound him with bronze shackles and took him to Babylon. In his distress he sought the favor of the LORD his God and humbled himself greatly before the God of his fathers. And when he prayed to him, the LORD was moved by his entreaty and listened to his plea; so he brought him back to Jerusalem and to his kingdom. Then Manasseh knew that the LORD is God.

Afterward he rebuilt the outer wall of the City of David, west of the Gihon spring in the valley, as far as the entrance of the Fish Gate and encircling the hill of Ophel; he also made it much higher. He stationed military commanders in all the fortified cities in Judah.

He got rid of the foreign gods and removed the image from the temple of the LORD, as well as all the altars he had built on the temple hill and in Jerusalem; and he threw them out of the city. Then he restored the altar of the LORD and sacrificed fellowship offerings and thank offerings on it, and told Judah to serve the LORD, the God of Israel.   —2 CHRONICLES 33:10–16

During his reign as king, Manasseh sacrificed his own children to idols, ruthlessly killed people, and practiced all kinds of evil. But after he repented and began to worship God, his conduct was radically altered.

Manasseh's life illustrates the truth that what we believe deep within us has a profound effect on our behavior. That's why the lawlessness and violence of our day should not surprise us. What can we expect from people when they have been taught that belief in God and absolute standards are mere superstitions? It's no wonder that cheating in our schools and teen pregnancy are national scandals. No wonder vicious crimes make the news every day.

The only real solution to this problem is a return to belief in God as He has revealed Himself in the Bible. Manasseh's life was dramatically changed, and the lives of people today are also transformed when they hear the truths of the Bible and respond in obedient faith.

Since what we believe is vital, we not only need the truths of God's Word that can save us from a Christless eternity, but we also need the truths that can prevent us from making tragic mistakes in this life. We need to keep fresh in our minds the beliefs that changed our lives.   —HERB VANDER LUGT

Erma's Legacy

Unless the LORD builds the house,
*   its builders labor in vain.*
Unless the LORD watches over the city,
*   the watchmen stand guard in vain.*
In vain you rise early
*   and stay up late,*
toiling for food to eat—
*   for he grants sleep to those he loves.*
Sons are a heritage from the LORD,
*   children a reward from him.*
Like arrows in the hands of a warrior
*   are sons born in one's youth.*
Blessed is the man
*   whose quiver is full of them.*
They will not be put to shame
*   when they contend with their enemies in the gate.*

—PSALM 127

*E*rma Bombeck is one of America's most well-loved writers. A homemaker, wife, and mother who writes about the foibles and follies of everyday existence in the home, Bombeck has parlayed her wit and wisdom into a successful syndicated newspaper column and a remarkable string of bestselling books.

Yet as she talks about her success, she is quick to remind people that her most important contribution is not becoming a millionaire author. Despite her fame and fortune, Erma Bombeck maintains, "My legacy is going to be [my] three kids."

In this day of quickly disintegrating values and sharply escalating social ills, that might be the most significant statement this woman of words has ever spoken. It gets to the root of so many problems in our modern society. For it is in the secure environment of the family that life's most valuable lessons are taught and learned.

As Christians who are trying to live by the precepts of God's Word, we need to reaffirm our commitment to our families. Sharing with them the gospel and God's guidelines for living must be more important to us than any of our own interests. Like Erma, we need to affirm that our family is our most important legacy.   —DAVE BRANON

The Parent Problem

Now I am ready to visit you for the third time, and I will not be a burden to you, because what I want is not your possessions but you. After all, children should not have to save up for their parents, but parents for their children. So I will very gladly spend for you everything I have and expend myself as well. If I love you more, will you love me less? Be that as it may, I have not been a burden to you. Yet, crafty fellow that I am, I caught you by trickery! Did I exploit you through any of the men I sent you? I urged Titus to go to you and I sent our brother with him. Titus did not exploit you, did he? Did we not act in the same spirit and follow the same course?

Have you been thinking all along that we have been defending ourselves to you? We have been speaking in the sight of God as those in Christ; and everything we do, dear friends, is for your strengthening. For I am afraid that when I come I may not find you as I want you to be, and you may not find me as you want me to be. I fear that there may be quarreling, jealousy, outbursts of anger, factions, slander, gossip, arrogance and disorder. I am afraid that when I come again my God will humble me before you, and I will be grieved over many who have sinned earlier and have not repented of the impurity, sexual sin and debauchery in which they have indulged. —2 Corinthians 12:14–21

Columnist Ann Landers asked parents, "If you had it to do over again, would you have children?" Of those who responded, 70 percent said no. When she published the results, many readers were surprised, angry, and confused. Some tried to explain away the percentage. They pointed out that those who had had a bad experience with a son or daughter would be most likely to write because this would allow them to vent their own frustrations. "Even so," says Miss Landers, "I was amazed by the number of people who confessed that having a family was not worth the trouble." She went on to comment that one reason for the disillusionment may be that couples enter parenthood with unrealistic expectations. "Everybody loves a cute little baby, but nobody wants a teenager who shoplifts or gets hooked on drugs."

It's also easy to romanticize about spiritual reproduction. The idea of leading someone to Christ is attractive. But what follows is often mixed with pain. We see this clearly in the apostle Paul's experience. He thought of himself as a parent to those he had brought to the Savior. But in the next breath he expressed sorrow over the mistakes and rebellion of their immature state. He knew some of the heartache of "bringing children into the world." Yet we never find him changing his mind about the value of preaching a message that results in the new birth.

Since Paul has long since gone to Heaven, the role of spiritual parenting has fallen to us. Let's not underestimate the sorrows or the joys of this challenging task, but keep right on—as he did.   —MART DE HAAN

Make Parenting a Priority!

*So if you faithfully obey the commands I am giving you today—
to love the LORD your God and to serve him with all your heart
and with all your soul—then I will send rain on your land in its
season, both autumn and spring rains, so that you may gather in
your grain, new wine and oil. I will provide grass in the fields for
your cattle, and you will eat and be satisfied.*

*Be careful, or you will be enticed to turn away and worship
other gods and bow down to them. Then the LORD's anger will
burn against you, and he will shut the heavens so that it will not
rain and the ground will yield no produce, and you will soon
perish from the good land the LORD is giving you. Fix these words
of mine in your hearts and minds; tie them as symbols on your
hands and bind them on your foreheads. Teach them to your children, talking about them when you sit at home and when you
walk along the road, when you lie down and when you get up.
Write them on the doorframes of your houses and on your gates,
so that your days and the days of your children may be many in
the land that the LORD swore to give your forefathers, as many as
the days that the heavens are above the earth.*

—DEUTERONOMY 11:13–21

*W*ith parenting, there are no trial runs. We have but one chance to be good parents, and that is now. A cartoon in the *Christian Herald* magazine vividly reminded me of this. It showed a mother sprawled out in an overstuffed chair, her hair disheveled and a frazzled look on her face. Toys and crayons cluttered the floor. A carpetsweeper was propped against the wall, and a dustcloth hung from her hand. As her husband came in from work, briefcase in hand, he gave her a quizzical look. Exhausted, she commented, "I'll be glad when the kids are grown so I'll have time to be a good parent."

Children are young only once, and that's when they need us most! Moses told Jewish parents to seize every opportunity to convey God's laws and precepts to their youngsters—when they sat down together, when they walked together, before they went to bed, and when they got up in the morning.

If a tidy house is more important than time out for the spontaneous interruption of children, perhaps housework should be left undone. If gaining and maintaining a high standard of living leaves no time for nurturing lives, then maybe the standard is too high. Today's fast pace of life, the pressure to succeed, and the lure of materialism all conspire to sap us of the emotional energy needed to build relationships with our children.

If this is true of you, sit down with your spouse and decide today to make parenting a priority.   —DENNIS DE HAAN

Keep 'Em Close

*Be careful, or you will be enticed to turn away and worship other gods and bow down to them. Then the L*ORD*'s anger will burn against you, and he will shut the heavens so that it will not rain and the ground will yield no produce, and you will soon perish from the good land the L*ORD *is giving you. Fix these words of mine in your hearts and minds; tie them as symbols on your hands and bind them on your foreheads. Teach them to your children, talking about them when you sit at home and when you walk along the road, when you lie down and when you get up. Write them on the doorframes of your houses and on your gates, so that your days and the days of your children may be many in the land that the L*ORD *swore to give your forefathers, as many as the days that the heavens are above the earth.*

—DEUTERONOMY 11:16–21

*M*y daughter Lisa was babysitting one night for Adam, Aubrey, and Alex. It was after 10:30, and she got bored. So she called home. For the next twenty minutes we talked about seventh grade, life, and Alex, who was teething. She had called to make herself feel better, but it was a pretty glad dad who got off the phone. It was nice to know that we can still share life as it comes. We can talk. We're still close.

I've been warned by enough parents to know that the next few years will be full of surprises. Will she call home "just to talk" in another year? In five years? Is the closeness permanent, or will walls replace bridges? I don't know. You can't really have a five-year plan for parenting. It's a day-to-day discipline. The goal every day is to keep our kids close—close to their Lord—close to the family.

This may have been where David failed with Absalom. First Kings 1:6 suggests that he lost touch with his son because he wasn't paying attention to what he was doing. He had not "interfered with him by asking, 'Why do you behave as you do?' " The lesson is clear: we must be involved in our children's lives.

Lord, don't let us become too busy to talk with our children, to play with them, to work with them. Help us keep them close, day after day after day.   —DAVE BRANON

A Pattern for Parents

O my people, hear my teaching;
*   listen to the words of my mouth.*
I will open my mouth in parables,
*   I will utter hidden things, things from of old—*
what we have heard and known,
*   what our fathers have told us.*
We will not hide them from their children;
*   we will tell the next generation*
the praiseworthy deeds of the LORD,
*   his power, and the wonders he has done.*
He decreed statutes for Jacob
*   and established the law in Israel,*
which he commanded our forefathers
*   to teach their children,*
so the next generation would know them,
*   even the children yet to be born,*
*   and they in turn would tell their children.*
Then they would put their trust in God
*   and would not forget his deeds*
*   but would keep his commands.*

*—*Psalm 78:1–7

A man was having a little chat with his young son. He was trying to tell him what a Christian should be like and how he should act. When he had finished talking his son looked at him and asked a stunning question. "Daddy," the boy wondered, "have I ever seen a Christian?" What a telling commentary on the life of that father!

How would we feel if our children were to respond to us in the same way? Psalm 78 gives us some help in making sure that doesn't happen. It sets forth a pattern for parenting—a method we can use to ensure that our children know the things of God and realize that we are people of God. According to Asaph, we can do this by "telling to the generation to come the praises of the Lord" (v. 4, NKJV). When we "make them known" (v. 5, NKJV) to our children, they will see by our words and our testimony that we are Christians.

Speaking of God's guidelines for living, Moses said, "Impress them on your children. Talk about them when you sit at home and when you walk along the road, when you lie down and when you get up" (Deuteronomy 6:7). By word and by personal example we must guide our children. In that way, we can show them and tell them what it means to be a Christian.

—PAUL VAN GORDER

Too Much to Do?

As Jesus and his disciples were on their way, he came to a village where a woman named Martha opened her home to him. She had a sister called Mary, who sat at the Lord's feet listening to what he said. But Martha was distracted by all the preparations that had to be made. She came to him and asked, "Lord, don't you care that my sister has left me to do the work by myself? Tell her to help me!"

"Martha, Martha," the Lord answered, "you are worried and upset about many things, but only one thing is needed. Mary has chosen what is better, and it will not be taken away from her."

—LUKE 10:38–42

I'm usually a happy person. I don't mind rolling with the punches, and I can take on as much work as anyone can give me. But not always. Some days there just seems to be too much to do. The schedule may seem so full of meetings, appointments, deadlines, and activities that there's no room to breathe. Life often contains too much work, parenting, home improvement, husbanding, and extracurricular responsibility for one person to handle.

When that happens to me—as I'm sure it happens to you—I have some options. I can retreat into a shell of inactivity and leave everyone who is depending on me out in the cold. I can slug my way through, moaning as I go and making everyone wish I had chosen option one. Or I can get my perspective realigned by reminding myself what Jesus said to Martha in today's Scripture passage.

Like many of us, Martha got so wrapped up in her service that she forgot the one thing that is most important—fellowship with her Lord. So Jesus had to remind her that she was neglecting the one thing that could never be taken away.

Are you overwhelmed? Don't lose sight of your priorities. Spend time with the Lord. He will lift your load and give you the right perspective.   —DAVE BRANON

Needed: Dads

Listen, my sons, to a father's instruction;
   pay attention and gain understanding.
I give you sound learning,
   so do not forsake my teaching.
When I was a boy in my father's house,
   still tender, and an only child of my mother,
he taught me and said,
   "Lay hold of my words with all your heart;
   keep my commands and you will live.
Get wisdom, get understanding;
   do not forget my words or swerve from them.
Do not forsake wisdom, and she will protect you;
   love her, and she will watch over you.
Wisdom is supreme; therefore get wisdom.
   Though it cost all you have, get understanding.
Esteem her, and she will exalt you;
   embrace her, and she will honor you.
She will set a garland of grace on your head
   and present you with a crown of splendor."
Listen, my son, accept what I say,
   and the years of your life will be many . . .
Hold on to instruction, do not let it go;
   guard it well, for it is your life. `

—PROVERBS 4:1–10, 13

*S*olomon knew from experience what it was like to have a father who cared. When he was young, his father had taken the time to instruct him in matters of wisdom and right living. Unfortunately, that is not happening in many homes today.

Josh McDowell has been trying to find out what dads are doing in Christian families, and the news isn't good. In his book *The Dad Difference*, McDowell reveals that there seems to be a parenting gap. These statistics are from McDowell's book:

- The average teen in our churches spends only two minutes a day in meaningful dialogue with his dad.
- Twenty-five percent of these teens say they have never had a meaningful conversation with their father—a talk centered on the teens' interests.

Solomon listened and learned when his father David took the initiative and instructed him as a child. What does taking the initiative mean for dads today? It means playing games with them, taking them places, hugging them, and talking with them. As Dad does these things, he opens up the lines of communication so he can teach his children about values, people, life, and God.

Children need Dad's instruction. Let's take the time to give them something worth listening to. —DAVE BRANON

Tennis and Parenting

Children, obey your parents in the Lord, for this is right. "Honor your father and mother"—which is the first commandment with a promise—"that it may go well with you and that you may enjoy long life on the earth."

Fathers, do not exasperate your children; instead, bring them up in the training and instruction of the Lord.

Slaves, obey your earthly masters with respect and fear, and with sincerity of heart, just as you would obey Christ. Obey them not only to win their favor when their eye is on you, but like slaves of Christ, doing the will of God from your heart. Serve wholeheartedly, as if you were serving the Lord, not men, because you know that the Lord will reward everyone for whatever good he does, whether he is slave or free.

And masters, treat your slaves in the same way. Do not threaten them, since you know that he who is both their Master and yours is in heaven, and there is no favoritism with him.

—EPHESIANS 6:1–9

*W*hat do tennis and parenting have in common? At first glance, not much. One is a game; the other is anything but a game. But there are certain similarities in the way the two tasks are carried out.

Tennis can be played two ways: with sportsmanship and graciousness, or with temper tantrums, "bashing" the officials, and bitter excuses.

Parents have similar options. They can concentrate on developing grace, self-control, and skill. Or they can make excuses by saying, "Sometimes I think I'm losing my mind. These kids are bringing out the worst in me. I know I shouldn't yell and scream, but I can't help it." Sound familiar?

Like successful tennis players, parents need a good coach—one who understands parenting's fine points, one who is experienced in self-control and unconditional love. We need Christ, the master teacher. Success is possible only when we seek His help and rely on Him. He said, "I am the vine; you are the branches. If a man remains in me and I in him, he will bear much fruit; apart from me you can do nothing" (John 15:5).

No, parenting isn't easy. Some tough shots may be fired at us. We may not win in straight sets. But Christ will help us to respond to our children with love and grace.

—MART DE HAAN

A Child's World

These commandments that I give you today are to be upon your hearts. Impress them on your children. Talk about them when you sit at home and when you walk along the road, when you lie down and when you get up. Tie them as symbols on your hands and bind them on your foreheads. Write them on the doorframes of your houses and on your gates . . .

In the future, when your son asks you, "What is the meaning of the stipulations, decrees and laws the LORD our God has commanded you?" tell him: "We were slaves of Pharaoh in Egypt, but the LORD brought us out of Egypt with a mighty hand. Before our eyes the LORD sent miraculous signs and wonders—great and terrible—upon Egypt and Pharaoh and his whole household. But he brought us out from there to bring us in and give us the land that he promised on oath to our forefathers. The LORD commanded us to obey all these decrees and to fear the LORD our God, so that we might always prosper and be kept alive, as is the case today. And if we are careful to obey all this law before the LORD our God, as he has commanded us, that will be our righteousness."
—DEUTERONOMY 6:6–9, 20–25

A popular pizza restaurant that caters to children advertises itself as "a place where a kid can be a kid." Actually, a child should be able to be a child anywhere.

But creating a child's world goes beyond letting a kid be a kid. Parents must understand their responsibilities in guiding that child. And for that we need to look at what the Bible says about parenting:

- Parents must teach God's truth (Deuteronomy 4:9; 32:46).
- Parents must lovingly discipline children because they are immature and need guidance (Proverbs 22:15; 29:15).
- Parents should not exasperate their children (Ephesians 6:4).
- Parents' wise decisions bring blessing to their children (Deuteronomy 30:19–20).
- Parents who are godly teach their children to obey (Ephesians 6:1; 1 Timothy 3:4).
- Parents who faithfully train their children can be confident that their efforts are not in vain (Proverbs 22:6).

Above all, to create a child's world, your home needs to be a place where you serve one another through God's love (Galatians 5:13). And it doesn't hurt to have some pizza now and then too!   —DAVE BRANON

Our Father's Love

"When Israel was a child, I loved him,
    and out of Egypt I called my son.
But the more I called Israel,
    the further they went from me.
They sacrificed to the Baals
    and they burned incense to images . . .
I led them with cords of human kindness,
    with ties of love;
I lifted the yoke from their neck
    and bent down to feed them . . .
"How can I give you up, Ephraim?
    How can I hand you over, Israel? . . .
My heart is changed within me;
    all my compassion is aroused.
I will not carry out my fierce anger,
    nor will I turn and devastate Ephraim . . .
They will follow the LORD; . . .
    his children will come trembling from the west.
They will come trembling
    like birds from Egypt,
    like doves from Assyria.
I will settle them in their homes,"
    declares the LORD.   —HOSEA 11:1–2, 4, 8–11

A young Christian dad took his parenting role seriously. When his son was an infant, he protected him. As the boy grew, his dad played ball with him, encouraged him, and tried to teach him about God and life. But in his teen years, the boy went too far and too fast in his move toward independence.

Like the prodigal son in Luke 15, he rejected his father's values. He made foolish decisions and got into trouble. The father was deeply disappointed, but he never gave up on him. "No matter what he's done," he said, "he's still my son. I'll never stop loving him. He'll always be welcome in my house." The joyful day finally came when father and son were reunited.

The people in Hosea's day followed a similar pattern. Although God had rescued them from Egypt and nourished them, they turned their backs on Him. They insulted His name by worshiping the gods of the Canaanites. But still God loved them and longed for their return (Hosea 11:8).

Do you fear that you may have strayed too far from God to be restored? He who saved and cares for you longs for your return. His arms are open in forgiveness and acceptance. He will never drive you away.

How glad we can be for our Father's love! —DAVE EGNER

A Mother's Wise Conduct

On the third day a wedding took place at Cana in Galilee. Jesus' mother was there, and Jesus and his disciples had also been invited to the wedding. When the wine was gone, Jesus' mother said to him, "They have no more wine."

"Dear woman, why do you involve me?" Jesus replied, "My time has not yet come."

His mother said to the servants, "Do whatever he tells you."

Nearby stood six stone water jars, the kind used by the Jews for ceremonial washing, each holding from twenty to thirty gallons.

Jesus said to the servants, "Fill the jars with water"; so they filled them to the brim.

Then he told them, "Now draw some out and take it to the master of the banquet."

They did so, and the master of the banquet tasted the water that had been turned into wine. He did not realize where it had come from, though the servants who had drawn the water knew . . .

This, the first of his miraculous signs, Jesus performed in Cana of Galilee. He thus revealed his glory, and his disciples put their faith in him.

—JOHN 2:1–11

I am reminded of one of the most pleasant duties I perform as a pastor. To visit the hospital and call on mothers of new babies is delightful because of the radiant happiness they display. Sometimes I engage in a bit of levity, telling them that motherhood will always be the best profession for women since it is entirely free from male competition. However, I also impress upon them their responsibility to rear their children in the fear and nurture of the Lord. Parenthood should be one of life's most rewarding experiences. However, it should remind us as well to seek God's help and guidance in the training of our little ones.

Today we call your attention to the blessed example set by Mary, the mother of our Savior. Although she couldn't understand some things Jesus said and did, she trusted Him fully, knowing He never made a mistake. She therefore instructed the servants at the wedding, who were in need of wine, to implicitly obey His every command. Her faith was rewarded, for Jesus immediately performed the miracle necessary to supply that which was lacking.

Mother, let Mary's wise faith be the guideline of your own conduct. Allow Jesus to control your life and aid you in handling the affairs of your household. The needs of your home—like those at the wedding in Cana—will be fully met if you heed Mary's words, "Do whatever he tells you."

—HERB VANDER LUGT

Right Behind Father

The proverbs of Solomon son of David, king of Israel:
   for attaining wisdom and discipline;
      for understanding words of insight;
   for acquiring a disciplined and prudent life,
      doing what is right and just and fair;
   for giving prudence to the simple,
      knowledge and discretion to the young—
   let the wise listen and add to their learning,
      and let the discerning get guidance—
   for understanding proverbs and parables,
      the sayings and riddles of the wise.
   The fear of the LORD is the beginning of knowledge,
      but fools despise wisdom and discipline.
   Listen, my son, to your father's instruction
      and do not forsake your mother's teaching.
   They will be a garland to grace your head
      and a chain to adorn your neck.

—PROVERBS 1:1–9

*I*t has been said, "A father's virtue is a child's best inheritance!" The greatest thing he can leave his family is a legacy of Christian example and unswerving devotion to the Lord. Such a radiant pattern of faithfulness to duty will serve as a beacon of guidance to his children as they make their way along treacherous paths of the world. His love and spirituality can enrich their lives and endow them with blessed memories more precious than anything he might bequeath them in his will. A good father first rules well his own life, and then with gracious understanding seeks to instruct and direct his children in the ways of righteousness.

A man and his young son were climbing a mountain when they came to a place where the ascent was especially difficult and dangerous. While the father paused to consider which way to go, the lad called out trustingly, "Choose the good path, Daddy; I'm coming right behind you!" These solemn words have a spiritual application. The head of the family bears a heavy responsibility. Being wrapped up in making a living, and having to take part in social and civic activities, he may easily neglect his sacred obligation to rear his children in the nurture and admonition of the Lord. It is indeed a challenging task to be a godly parent.

May we as Christian fathers dedicate ourselves anew to our high and holy calling! May we set the right course, knowing that young lives are always right behind us!   —HENRY BOSCH

Hey, Dad!

Sons are a heritage from the LORD,
   children a reward from him.
Like arrows in the hands of a warrior
   are sons born in one's youth.
Blessed is the man
   whose quiver is full of them.
They will not be put to shame
   when they contend with their enemies in the gate.
Blessed are all who fear the LORD,
   who walk in his ways.
You will eat the fruit of your labor;
   blessings and prosperity will be yours.
Your wife will be like a fruitful vine
   within your house;
your sons will be like olive shoots
   around your table.
Thus is the man blessed
   who fears the LORD.

—PSALM 127:3–128:4

*S*ometimes when I'm in a crowded place, such as in a mall or at a ballgame, I hear someone call out, "Hey, Dad!" I instinctively look around to see who's calling. Although most of the time it's not one of my children, I'm always reminded of the universal nature of the name Dad. It's a one-size-fits-all label.

I'm also reminded of the incredible responsibility we fathers have—and of the great privilege. All of us who answer to "Hey, Dad!" have at least one child who looks to us for protection, love, guidance, friendship, training, discipline, and so much more.

I must say that I can't think of a more rewarding job. Being a dad means that God has entrusted me with the task of training my children in the way they should go (Proverbs 22:6). He has given me the duty to teach them the fear of the Lord (Psalm 128). He has asked me to bring them up in the training and instruction of the Lord without exasperating them (Ephesians 6:4). He has allowed me to share the heritage of faith. And for my efforts I get lots of hugs and kisses, really neat Father's Day cards, and the chance to hear, "Hey, Dad!"

God knows the responsibilities and joys of fatherhood because He's our heavenly Father. And as our Father He will give us what we need to care for our children.

—DAVE BRANON

The Task of Molding Children

Children, obey your parents in the Lord, for this is right. "Honor your father and mother"—which is the first commandment with a promise—"that it may go well with you and that you may enjoy long life on the earth."

Fathers, do not exasperate your children; instead, bring them up in the training and instruction of the Lord.

—EPHESIANS 6:1–4

*E*ducators, psychologists, and behaviorial experts have confirmed the startling fact that a child attains his basic personality structure by the time he is four or five years old. In other words, many adult characteristics are already determined at an early age! Since the home is the place where your youngster makes his first contact with reality, your role as parent is of utmost importance. You are his first and most influential teacher, guide, example, and loving critic. How vital it is to bring up your child "in the training and instruction of the Lord"! (Ephesians 6:4).

Canon Shore writes, "I once saw, lying side by side in a sculptor's workshop, two heads made of metal. One was perfect. All the features of a manly, noble face were clear and distinct. The other, however, had scarcely a single, recognizable human characteristic. It was marred and spoiled. The man who was showing it to me said, 'This one is badly distorted because the metal was allowed to cool before it was stamped out, and therefore it wouldn't take the impression.' So, too, many souls might have been stamped with the likeness of the Savior while they were still warm with the glow of early youth, but they were allowed to become cold. Thus, they were misformed and their lives ruined."

Christian parent, ask yourself, "What impression am I having upon the little ones God has placed in my home? Am I loving and training them correctly?" By word and example we must all try to mold our children so they will grow up to walk in "the way of the Lord"!

—HENRY BOSCH

The Making of a Masterpiece

These are the commands, decrees and laws the LORD your God directed me to teach you to observe in the land that you are crossing the Jordan to possess, so that you, your children and their children after them may fear the LORD your God as long as you live by keeping all his decrees and commands that I give you, and so that you may enjoy long life. Hear, O Israel, and be careful to obey so that it may go well with you and that you may increase greatly in a land flowing with milk and honey, just as the LORD, the God of your fathers, promised you.

Hear, O Israel: The LORD our God, the LORD is one. Love the LORD your God with all your heart and with all your soul and with all your strength. These commandments that I give you today are to be upon your hearts. Impress them on your children. Talk about them when you sit at home and when you walk along the road, when you lie down and when you get up. Tie them as symbols on your hands and bind them on your foreheads. Write them on the doorframes of your houses and on your gates.

—DEUTERONOMY 6:1–9

Children do not automatically become model men and women. Their development must be carefully nurtured. Raising children calls for patience, diligence, determination, wise instruction, and loving correction.

A friend called on Michelangelo as he was putting what appeared to be the finishing touches on a sculpture. Later when the visitor stopped in to see the artist again, he was surprised to find him busy on the same statue. Seeing no evident changes, he exclaimed, "You haven't been working on that statue all this time, have you!" "Yes, I have," the sculptor replied. "I've been busy retouching this part, and polishing that part; I have softened this feature, and brought out that muscle; I've given more expression to the lips, and more energy to that arm." "But all those things are so insignificant," said his visitor. "They are mere trifles." "That may be so," replied Michelangelo, "but trifles make perfection, and perfection is no trifle."

The training of a child demands that same kind of diligence. By reading the Bible, telling its stories, praying, and teaching "line upon line," parents must day after day shape and mold the character of their children so that they will choose to be like Christ.

Yes, the proper training of a child is the making of a masterpiece.

—RICHARD DE HAAN

Indispensable

Paul, an apostle of Christ Jesus by the will of God, according to the promise of life that is in Christ Jesus,

To Timothy, my dear son:

Grace, mercy and peace from God the Father and Christ Jesus our Lord.

I thank God, whom I serve, as my forefathers did, with a clear conscience, as night and day I constantly remember you in my prayers. Recalling your tears, I long to see you, so that I may be filled with joy. I have been reminded of your sincere faith, which first lived in your grandmother Lois and in your mother Eunice and, I am persuaded, now lives in you also.

—2 TIMOTHY 1:1–5

A talented stay-at-home mother wrote a delightful essay in which she vividly describes (without complaining) the frustrations, sacrifices, and loneliness that accompany her chosen lifestyle. It's not glamorous to deal with a fussy eighteen-month-old who is teething, to settle quarrels between an irrational three-year-old and a pushy five-year old, and to listen to the incessant chatter of small children. Yet she concludes that her role is indispensable for the total well-being of her children. How true!

The importance of a godly mother's role in the life of a child cannot be overemphasized. Think of Timothy, for example, the young man the apostle Paul considered his spiritual son and a valuable partner in ministry. In his second letter to him, Paul recalled how Timothy had been influenced by "the genuine faith" of his grandmother Lois and his mother Eunice (2 Timothy 1:5). God used two generations of loving mothers to prepare Timothy for the crucial work he would have in spreading the gospel and establishing congregations of believers in Christ.

Let's praise the Lord for mothers who not only care for their children physically but also nurture them spiritually. Mothers like that are indispensable!   —HERB VANDER LUGT

The Greatest Heritage

These are the commands, decrees and laws the LORD your God directed me to teach you to observe in the land that you are crossing the Jordan to possess, so that you, your children and their children after them may fear the LORD your God as long as you live by keeping all his decrees and commands that I give you, and so that you may enjoy long life. Hear, O Israel, and be careful to obey so that it may go well with you and that you may increase greatly in a land flowing with milk and honey, just as the LORD, the God of your fathers, promised you.

Hear, O Israel: The LORD our God, the LORD is one. Love the LORD your God with all your heart and with all your soul and with all your strength. These commandments that I give you today are to be upon your hearts. Impress them on your children. Talk about them when you sit at home and when you walk along the road, when you lie down and when you get up. Tie them as symbols on your hands and bind them on your foreheads. Write them on the doorframes of your houses and on your gates.

—DEUTERONOMY 6:1–9

Having children is a great blessing, but their training entails a tremendous responsibility! Parents are to teach their youngsters to love God, to respect authority, and to shun evil. One of the best ways to do that is to have daily devotions in the home.

Courtland Myers, in a spiritual and nostalgic mood, wrote, "I am back here now on the banks of the Hudson River in the rustic farmhouse where I lived for so many years. To my memory comes a picture of the old kitchen and its great fireplace, where Father, Mother, and we twelve children met twice a day for our family altar. I shall never forget the marvelous influence that was wielded in my life by my father reading the Bible and then lifting his heart in earnest prayer to the Lord. It shouldn't surprise you when I tell you that every one of those children, including myself, was saved by the grace of God. Four of them today are ministers of Jesus Christ. The others became Sunday school teachers and are also serving the Savior in various honorable professions. And we found our inspiration and new life in Christ when we unitedly worshiped the Lord in that old home twice a day. The greatest blessing one can ever have is the spiritual power and moral uplift of such an environment. My father and mother were never able to leave me a dollar, but they did leave me the greatest riches in the world—a Christian heritage!"

Are you bringing up your children in the "training and instruction of the Lord"? (Ephesians 6:4). It's the greatest legacy you can bestow on them.   —HENRY BOSCH

The Love That Disciplines

And you have forgotten that word of encouragement that addresses you as sons:

"My son, do not make light of the Lord's discipline, and do not lose heart when he rebukes you, because the Lord disciplines those he loves, and he punishes everyone he accepts as a son."

Endure hardship as discipline; God is treating you as sons. For what son is not disciplined by his father? If you are not disciplined (and everyone undergoes discipline), then you are illegitimate children and not true sons. Moreover, we have all had human fathers who disciplined us and we respected them for it. How much more should we submit to the Father of our spirits and live! Our fathers disciplined us for a little while as they thought best; but God disciplines us for our good, that we may share in his holiness. No discipline seems pleasant at the time, but painful. Later on, however, it produces a harvest of righteousness and peace for those who have been trained by it.

Therefore, strengthen your feeble arms and weak knees. "Make level paths for your feet," so that the lame may not be disabled, but rather healed. —Hebrews 12:5–13

*A*ll of us would rather enjoy life's blessings than face its trials. Yet both are part of our lives, and our heavenly Father knows exactly how much of each is appropriate for us. Everything He allows into our lives comes from His heart of love.

Here is how one writer has described the balance between mercy and discipline. "The Christian life is like the dial of a clock. The hands are God's hands, passing over and over again—the short hand of discipline and the long hand of mercy. Slowly and surely the hand of discipline must pass, and God speaks at each stroke. But over and over passes the hand of mercy, showering down a twelvefold blessing for each stroke of discipline and trial. Both hands are fastened to one secure pivot: the great unchanging heart of our God of love."

Since "no discipline seems pleasant at the time, but painful" (Hebrews 12:11), why can't God leave out the discipline, the "child training," we might ask. The answer is simple. If He were to do that, our spiritual growth would be stunted. We need every trial because each is designed by God to help us mature and to conform us to the image of His Son.

So don't become discouraged when you face life's difficulties. God has an infinite, perfect plan for you. From His eternal hand of everlasting love come both the discipline that shapes you and the mercy that comforts you. Yes, it is His love that disciplines. —Paul Van Gorder

A Dad Who Didn't Quit

Children, obey your parents in the Lord, for this is right. "Honor your father and mother"—which is the first commandment with a promise—"that it may go well with you and that you may enjoy long life on the earth."

Fathers, do not exasperate your children; instead, bring them up in the training and instruction of the Lord.

—EPHESIANS 6:1–4

*T*hree months before my father died of cancer, he wrote me a letter. I had just left the security of teaching and had gone into fulltime freelance writing. Life was very uncertain.

Dad said, "I know you, I know what's behind you, and I am pretty sure that I understand your goals and the kind of writing you hope to do and the message you wish to convey. Stay in there, and may the Lord bless you. If you ever get in a tight place and need some ready cash, let me know. I think I know where I can lay my hands on a little of it."

When Dad sent me that letter, I was thirty-six years old and had a wife and three children. But I was still his son and he knew I needed encouragement. He was still parenting, in the best sense of the word.

When the Bible tells fathers to bring up their children "in the training and instruction of the Lord" (Ephesians 6:4), it doesn't put a time limit on the process. As children grow, a parent's role changes, but the responsibility to care remains the same. Loving, training, admonishing, and encouraging never go out of style.

I still have that letter. I'm still thankful for the man who never stopped being my dad.   —David McCasland

Apprenticeship Program

For it seems to me that God has put us apostles on display at the end of the procession, like men condemned to die in the arena. We have been made a spectacle to the whole universe, to angels as well as to men. We are fools for Christ, but you are so wise in Christ! We are weak, but you are strong! You are honored, we are dishonored! To this very hour we go hungry and thirsty, we are in rags, we are brutally treated, we are homeless. We work hard with our own hands. When we are cursed, we bless; when we are persecuted, we endure it; when we are slandered, we answer kindly. Up to this moment we have become the scum of the earth, the refuse of the world.

I am not writing this to shame you, but to warn you, as my dear children. Even though you have ten thousand guardians in Christ, you do not have many fathers, for in Christ Jesus I became your father through the gospel. Therefore I urge you to imitate me.
—1 CORINTHIANS 4:9–16

*L*ife certainly was a lot simpler years ago. If a man was a carpenter, his son was likely to be the same. That's because the shop was at home and the boy worked with his father. The son watched carefully as Dad cut the wood, planed and smoothed it, then fastened it together to build a table or a bench. It was apprenticeship by example.

Most young people don't learn their trades like that anymore. Vocations are far too complex and the training way too demanding.

One aspect of life, however, is the same as it was years ago. Children not only learned how to do things from Dad and Mom, they also learned about life. They saw their parents' values and ethics in action every day in their homes.

Christian moms and dads still have "little apprentices" watching how they put their beliefs into practice. It goes on at mealtime, in the car, in the store, in conversation with or about neighbors—all the time. What a wonderful opportunity to teach our children how to live for Christ! And young people not only need it, they want it.

Paul told his children in the faith to imitate him—to follow his example (1 Corinthians 4:16). Are we living for Christ in such a way that we want our children to imitate us?

—DAVE EGNER

Little Cucumbers

These commandments that I give you today are to be upon your hearts. Impress them on your children. Talk about them when you sit at home and when you walk along the road, when you lie down and when you get up. Tie them as symbols on your hands and bind them on your foreheads. Write them on the doorframes of your houses and on your gates.

When the LORD your God brings you into the land he swore to your fathers, to Abraham, Isaac and Jacob, to give you—a land with large, flourishing cities you did not build, houses filled with all kinds of good things you did not provide, wells you did not dig, and vineyards and olive groves you did not plant—then when you eat and are satisfied, be careful that you do not forget the LORD, who brought you out of Egypt, out of the land of slavery.   —DEUTERONOMY 6:6–12

When I was just a boy, I was intrigued by a large cucumber. It was no different from any other cucumber, but it was in the strangest place. My uncle kept it in a bottle on a shelf. This particular cucumber was many times too large to go through the neck of the bottle. I wondered how it got there in the first place.

I was filled with awe of my uncle who could perform such a feat. He joked about it and never told me how he did it. My mother finally explained that when the cucumber was very tiny, it had been passed through the narrow neck and allowed to grow while still attached to the vine.

My mother practiced a similar principle with her children. From my earliest memory she surrounded me with prayer and instruction and the gospel. As a result, I was brought to Christ and am now safe in the bottle of His salvation.

What a lesson for parents who have "little cucumbers" at home. Don't let anything interfere with your first duty toward them. The person who said "Give me a child till he is seven and I care not who gets him after that" knew the value of early training.

Don't neglect your little cucumbers. Soon they will be big.

—M. R. De Haan

Spelling Problems

You, however, know all about my teaching, my way of life, my purpose, faith, patience, love, endurance, persecutions, sufferings—what kinds of things happened to me in Antioch, Iconium and Lystra, the persecutions I endured. Yet the Lord rescued me from all of them. In fact, everyone who wants to live a godly life in Christ Jesus will be persecuted, while evil men and impostors will go from bad to worse, deceiving and being deceived. But as for you, continue in what you have learned and have become convinced of, because you know those from whom you learned it, and how from infancy you have known the holy Scriptures, which are able to make you wise for salvation through faith in Christ Jesus. All Scripture is God-breathed and is useful for teaching, rebuking, correcting and training in righteousness, so that the man of God may be thoroughly equipped for every good work.

—2 TIMOTHY 3:10–17

My mother was moving from the house we had called home for thirty-six years, and we were cleaning out the treasures. As I rummaged through my stuff, I discovered something I felt would be instructive for Steve, my ten-year-old fifth-grader. It was my old fifth-grade spelling book. I thought I would show him how much tougher things were back in those days. But when Steve and I later compared his book with mine, we agreed that his words were harder!

As I considered this, I began to think about the culture in which our children are growing up. It is not just spelling that is harder. Life itself has added layers of toughness since my school days.

With so much overt sinfulness being pushed a child's way, it could be harder to resist temptation and to do what is right. New negative influences challenge a young person as he tries to make wise choices.

Yet the answer is the same as it has always been. "From infancy you have known the holy Scriptures"—that was how Paul characterized Timothy's training (2 Timothy 3:15). This is still the way it should be for our children. No matter how tough the times, the solutions are always spelled out in God's Word. It's one book that never changes. —DAVE BRANON

Is Jesus Exclusive?

"Do not let your hearts be troubled. Trust in God; trust also in me. In my Father's house are many rooms; if it were not so, I would have told you. I am going there to prepare a place for you. And if I go and prepare a place for you, I will come back and take you to be with me that you also may be where I am. You know the way to the place where I am going."

Thomas said to him, "Lord, we don't know where you are going, so how can we know the way?"

Jesus answered, "I am the way and the truth and the life. No one comes to the Father except through me. If you really knew me, you would know my Father as well. From now on, you do know him and have seen him."

—JOHN 14:1–7

I once saw Billy Graham's daughter Anne Graham Lotz on a popular news talk program. The interviewer asked, "Are you one of those who believe that Jesus is exclusively the only way to heaven?" He added, "You know how mad that makes people these days!" Without blinking she replied, "Jesus is not exclusive. He died so that anyone could come to Him for salvation."

What a great response! Christianity is not an exclusive club limited to an elite few who fit the perfect profile. Everyone is welcome regardless of color, class, or clout.

In spite of this wonderful reality, Christ's claim in John 14:6 to be the only way to God continues to offend. Yet Jesus is the only way—the only option that works. All of us are guilty before God. We are sinners and cannot help ourselves. Our sin had to be dealt with. Jesus, as God in the flesh, died to pay the penalty for our sins and then rose from the dead. No other religious leader offers what Jesus provides in His victory over sin and death.

The gospel of Christ is offensive to some, but it is the wonderful truth that God loves us enough to come and take care of our biggest problem—sin. And as long as sin is the problem, the world needs Jesus! —JOE STOWELL

Smart Dad

My son, pay attention to what I say;
    listen closely to my words.
Do not let them out of your sight,
    keep them within your heart;
for they are life to those who find them
    and health to a man's whole body.
Above all else, guard your heart,
    for it is the wellspring of life.
Put away perversity from your mouth;
    keep corrupt talk far from your lips.
Let your eyes look straight ahead,
    fix your gaze directly before you.
Make level paths for your feet
    and take only ways that are firm.
Do not swerve to the right or the left;
    keep your foot from evil.

—PROVERBS 4:20–27

A hard-working single dad named William Jackson Smart was the inspiration for the creation of Father's Day. His wife died in 1898 while giving birth to their sixth child, and the Civil War veteran was left to raise the children alone in rural Washington.

In May 1909, Smart's daughter, by then a married woman named Sonora Dodd, heard a sermon enumerating the virtues of motherhood. It was Mother's Day, a new American holiday that had begun the previous year. Sonora decided to honor her dad's dedication to his children by seeking to have a Father's Day designated on the calendar. The day caught on, but it wasn't permanently established as an annual holiday in the United States until 1972.

What a vital role fathers can play in the home as they train their children to follow God's ways! Proverbs 4 gives these nuggets of wisdom that dads can pass on to their children: "Do not set foot on the path of the wicked" (v. 14). "Guard your heart" (v. 23). "Put away perversity from your mouth" (v. 24). And finally, "Keep your foot from evil" (v. 27).

We honor our godly fathers by obeying their instruction. And we should pray for all dads to recognize their God-given role of training in the home.   —DAVE BRANON

A Masterpiece

For Christ's love compels us, because we are convinced that one died for all, and therefore all died. And he died for all, that those who live should no longer live for themselves but for him who died for them and was raised again.

So from now on we regard no one from a worldly point of view. Though we once regarded Christ in this way, we do so no longer. Therefore, if anyone is in Christ, he is a new creation; the old has gone, the new has come! All this is from God, who reconciled us to himself through Christ and gave us the ministry of reconciliation: that God was reconciling the world to himself in Christ, not counting men's sins against them. And he has committed to us the message of reconciliation. We are therefore Christ's ambassadors, as though God were making his appeal through us. We implore you on Christ's behalf: Be reconciled to God. God made him who had no sin to be sin for us, so that in him we might become the righteousness of God.

—2 CORINTHIANS 5:14–21

One of my earliest memories of my dad is that he loved doing paint-by-number pictures. The canvas was large, but the numbered segments where a predetermined color would go were very small. Dad would sit in his chair in our basement for hours, working meticulously with his painting in front of him and a cup of coffee at his side.

As a boy, I would sit on the basement stairs and watch with fascination. My interest did not stem from a misguided thought that doing paint-by-number work made my dad a great artist. Rather, I was amazed at how patiently he would work on each painting. Finally, the thousands of slivers of color became an image that Dad considered well worth the effort.

As I think of my dad's patience in bringing a painting to life, my heart is directed to our heavenly Father. He looks on us and sees the voids and imperfections in our lives, yet lovingly and patiently does His work in us to make us His master-piece—a masterpiece that "conform[s] to the likeness of His Son" (Romans 8:29). —BILL CROWDER

A Dad Looks Back

Listen, my sons, to a father's instruction;
pay attention and gain understanding.
I give you sound learning,
so do not forsake my teaching . . .
Get wisdom, get understanding;
do not forget my words or swerve from them.
Do not forsake wisdom, and she will protect you;
love her, and she will watch over you.
Wisdom is supreme; therefore get wisdom.
Though it cost all you have, get understanding.
Esteem her, and she will exalt you;
embrace her, and she will honor you.
She will set a garland of grace on your head
and present you with a crown of splendor."
Listen, my son, accept what I say,
and the years of your life will be many.
I guide you in the way of wisdom
and lead you along straight paths.
When you walk, your steps will not be hampered;
when you run, you will not stumble.
Hold on to instruction, do not let it go;
guard it well, for it is your life.

—PROVERBS 4:1–2, 5–13

*W*here did two decades go? How could they have sneaked by so fast? How could my little girl with the ringlet hair and cherubic smile already be twenty years old?

Wasn't it just a short time ago that she learned to write her name? Now she's writing term papers and e-mail. Wasn't it just yesterday that she sat on her tricycle and asked Jesus to be her Savior? Now she's working with foster kids to tell them of Christ.

Gone are the preschool years, the elementary years, and now the teenage years. With the loss comes the recollection of so many great times—so many opportunities to reveal God's goodness, His guidelines, His love, and His salvation to Lisa.

As I think back on the opportunities I had during her formative years, I've concluded that the most vital aspect of parenting is relationship. Only when we maintain close fellowship with our children can we instruct them properly. When parents and their children share a relationship of mutual respect, new moments of teaching build themselves into a lifetime of love and strong values.

Mom and Dad, make it easier for your children to listen to your teaching by nourishing the relationship. It will help to make looking back a great experience. —Dave Branon

Trapped!

At that time Jesus said, "I praise you, Father, Lord of heaven and earth, because you have hidden these things from the wise and learned, and revealed them to little children. Yes, Father, for this was your good pleasure.

"All things have been committed to me by my Father. No one knows the Son except the Father, and no one knows the Father except the Son and those to whom the Son chooses to reveal him.

"Come to me, all you who are weary and burdened, and I will give you rest. Take my yoke upon you and learn from me, for I am gentle and humble in heart, and you will find rest for your souls. For my yoke is easy and my burden is light."

—MATTHEW 11:25–30

New York City man who sold books and magazines on the street was freed after being trapped for two days under a mountain of paper in his apartment. The man's collection of printed materials, which he had stacked wall to wall and floor to ceiling, collapsed and buried him alive. Emergency workers filled fifty garbage bags as they dug through the debris just to reach him.

We don't need a Mount Everest of old newspapers to know the feeling of being trapped under the crush of our work and the burden of overwhelming spiritual demands. Yet a glance at our Savior reveals His deep inner rest. In *Tyranny of the Urgent*, Charles E. Hummel writes: "Jesus' prayerful waiting for God's instructions . . . gave Him a sense of direction, set a steady pace, and enabled Him to do every task God assigned."

Jesus invites the weary to come to Him. "Take my yoke upon you and learn from me, for I am gentle and humble in heart, and you will find rest for your souls" (Matthew 11:29).

This rest that comes with salvation is not achieved by effort but is received by faith. In Christ we can also find release from the tyranny of the urgent and accomplish everything He has given us to do. —DAVID MCCASLAND

The Transaction

As for you, you were dead in your transgressions and sins, in which you used to live when you followed the ways of this world and of the ruler of the kingdom of the air, the spirit who is now at work in those who are disobedient. All of us also lived among them at one time, gratifying the cravings of our sinful nature and following its desires and thoughts. Like the rest, we were by nature objects of wrath. But because of his great love for us, God, who is rich in mercy, made us alive with Christ even when we were dead in transgressions—it is by grace you have been saved. And God raised us up with Christ and seated us with him in the heavenly realms in Christ Jesus, in order that in the coming ages he might show the incomparable riches of his grace, expressed in his kindness to us in Christ Jesus. For it is by grace you have been saved, through faith—and this not from yourselves, it is the gift of God—not by works, so that no one can boast. For we are God's workmanship, created in Christ Jesus to do good works, which God prepared in advance for us to do. —Ephesians 2:1–10*

*C*an more than half of the adult population in the United States be wrong? A survey by the Barna Research Group recently revealed that 54 percent say that people who are generally good and do enough good things for others will earn a place in heaven. That is just one of many methods people suggest as ways to merit entrance into God's eternal kingdom.

Let's think about what has to happen for a person to get to heaven, and why the "good works" idea falls short.

First, we must recognize that we are all born spiritually dead. In Ephesians 2:1, we are taught that we "were dead in . . . transgressions and sins." The spiritual aspect of our existence was dead on arrival when we were physically born into this world. That soul, however, can be made alive. Paul described it like this: "For as in Adam all die, so in Christ all will be made alive" (1 Corinthians 15:22).

To be made alive, a transaction must take place. Something specific has to happen to turn what was dead into something alive. It is not triggered by good works but happens only when, by faith, you accept God's gift of salvation (2 Corinthians 6:2; Ephesians 2:8).

Is your soul alive today? If not, make the transaction and accept God's wonderful gift. —DAVE BRANON

Michael's Baptism

People were bringing little children to Jesus to have him touch them, but the disciples rebuked them. When Jesus saw this, he was indignant. He said to them, "Let the little children come to me, and do not hinder them, for the kingdom of God belongs to such as these. I tell you the truth, anyone who will not receive the kingdom of God like a little child will never enter it." And he took the children in his arms, put his hands on them and blessed them. —MARK 10:13–16

*M*ichael wanted to be baptized. At first his father had reservations about this because Michael is autistic. Autism is a developmental disability that affects a person's social interaction and communication skills.

There was no question that thirty-five-year-old Michael had trusted Jesus for salvation, and the church leadership enthusiastically approved his baptism. But he would have to stand in front of the entire congregation.

Knowing that Michael didn't like surprises, his dad reviewed all that would happen. But during the baptism, when the pastor said, "Michael, I baptize you in the name of the Father," Michael interrupted as if to remind him, "and the Son!" The congregation smiled with joy. And Michael was baptized in obedience to Christ's command.

Each of us comes to Jesus at a different level of spiritual understanding, and Jesus extends His welcome to all who respond. When little children approached the Savior, His disciples tried to send them away. But Christ rebuked them and said, "Let the little children come to me" (Mark 10:14). And that also applies to the developmentally disabled.

The gospel is simple. The Savior is approachable. And His invitation is open to everyone. —DENNIS FISHER

Taking God at His Word

This is the one who came by water and blood—Jesus Christ. He did not come by water only, but by water and blood. And it is the Spirit who testifies, because the Spirit is the truth. For there are three that testify: the Spirit, the water and the blood; and the three are in agreement. We accept man's testimony, but God's testimony is greater because it is the testimony of God, which he has given about his Son. Anyone who believes in the Son of God has this testimony in his heart. Anyone who does not believe God has made him out to be a liar, because he has not believed the testimony God has given about his Son. And this is the testimony: God has given us eternal life, and this life is in his Son. He who has the Son has life; he who does not have the Son of God does not have life.

I write these things to you who believe in the name of the Son of God so that you may know that you have eternal life.

—1 JOHN 5:6–13

*M*any true believers in Christ are plagued with doubt about their salvation. Even though they have come in repentance and faith to Jesus as their Savior, they still wonder, "Will I really go to heaven?"

My late husband, Bill, often told about something that happened to him when he was two years old. One day he disobediently wandered from home and got lost. When his parents realized that he was missing, they went out searching for him. Finally, to everyone's immense relief, they spotted their tearful boy and carried him safely home.

Days later, Billy overheard his mother relate this incident to a visitor. When she reached the part where they went out searching for him, Billy began to relive the story. "Mommy, Mommy!" he sobbed. "Did you ever find me?" Surprised and deeply touched by his doubt, she embraced him and said, "Of course, my child! Don't you remember that happy moment? See, you're with us now, and we'll make sure that you always are." That comforted Billy, because he took her at her word.

The New Testament letter of 1 John was written to give believers the assurance of salvation. That assurance can be yours as you take God at His word. —JOANIE YODER

Keeping It Simple

When I came to you, brothers, I did not come with eloquence or superior wisdom as I proclaimed to you the testimony about God. For I resolved to know nothing while I was with you except Jesus Christ and him crucified. I came to you in weakness and fear, and with much trembling. My message and my preaching were not with wise and persuasive words, but with a demonstration of the Spirit's power, so that your faith might not rest on men's wisdom, but on God's power.

We do, however, speak a message of wisdom among the mature, but not the wisdom of this age or of the rulers of this age, who are coming to nothing. No, we speak of God's secret wisdom, a wisdom that has been hidden and that God destined for our glory before time began. None of the rulers of this age understood it, for if they had, they would not have crucified the Lord of glory. However, as it is written:

> *"No eye has seen,*
> *no ear has heard,*
> *no mind has conceived*
> *what God has prepared for those who love him"—*

but God has revealed it to us by his Spirit.
The Spirit searches all things, even the deep things of God.

—1 Corinthians 2:1–10

*W*riting for a Grand Rapids newspaper, columnist Cathy Runyon offered a pocket guide to "parentese." While many consider parenting to be a long-term commitment, she humorously notes that often it's more like a "short sentence": "Wash your hands. Brush your teeth. Comb your hair. Clip your nails. Take a bath. Remember the deodorant. Get a haircut. Polish your shoes. Change your clothes. Button your shirt. Don't pick it. Shut the door. Clean your room. Make your bed. Do your homework. Flush the toilet. Do your chores. Stop that noise. Save your money. Write to Grandma. Phone home first. Beware of strangers. No more television. Wait till Christmas."

While acknowledging the depth of the wisdom of Christ, the apostle Paul also emphasized the simplicity of his approach to spiritual parenting. He proclaimed a message that we in turn can put in simple sentences: "Jesus loves you. He was crucified. He is risen. He is Lord. We have sinned. We need forgiveness. Don't trust yourself. Believe in Him. Let Him lead. Depart from sin. Help one another. Spread the word—Jesus has come. He's coming again."

Father, help us to grow to spiritual maturity but never forget those simple truths. —Mart De Haan

Equipped for the Task

After the death of Moses the servant of the LORD, the LORD said to Joshua son of Nun, Moses' aide: . . . As I was with Moses, so I will be with you; I will never leave you nor forsake you.

"Be strong and courageous, because you will lead these people to inherit the land I swore to their forefathers to give them. Be strong and very courageous. Be careful to obey all the law my servant Moses gave you; do not turn from it to the right or to the left, that you may be successful wherever you go. Do not let this Book of the Law depart from your mouth; meditate on it day and night, so that you may be careful to do everything written in it. Then you will be prosperous and successful. Have I not commanded you? Be strong and courageous. Do not be terrified; do not be discouraged, for the LORD your God will be with you wherever you go."

—JOSHUA 1:1, 5–9

I was in England during World War II working as a surgical technician in an army hospital when I heard the shocking radio announcement: "Franklin Delano Roosevelt is dead!" I was saddened and troubled. Was Vice President Harry Truman qualified to be president?

I was relieved when I heard him say that he felt as if an enormous weight had fallen on his shoulders and that he desired people everywhere to pray for him. This reassured me that he humbly recognized his inadequacies and his need for God's help.

Few of us will ever be thrust into a position of leadership with duties of that magnitude, but most of us know the feeling of inadequacy in the face of a great responsibility we are about to assume. It might be that of taking on a new job, getting a promotion at work, choosing a spouse, becoming a parent, or accepting a new ministry in Sunday school or church.

When we face a new challenge, we can take courage from the Lord's words to Joshua (1:9). We can accept our opportunity as from Him and believe that He will give us all we need to do it well. If we meditate on His Word, obey it, prayerfully rely on Him, and work diligently, He will do the rest. He will equip us for the task.

—HERB VANDER LUGT

Instructed by God

These are the commands, decrees and laws the LORD your God directed me to teach you to observe in the land that you are crossing the Jordan to possess, so that you, your children and their children after them may fear the LORD your God as long as you live by keeping all his decrees and commands that I give you, and so that you may enjoy long life. Hear, O Israel, and be careful to obey so that it may go well with you and that you may increase greatly in a land flowing with milk and honey, just as the LORD, the God of your fathers, promised you.

Hear, O Israel: The LORD our God, the LORD is one. Love the LORD your God with all your heart and with all your soul and with all your strength. These commandments that I give you today are to be upon your hearts. Impress them on your children. Talk about them when you sit at home and when you walk along the road, when you lie down and when you get up. Tie them as symbols on your hands and bind them on your foreheads. Write them on the doorframes of your houses and on your gates.

—DEUTERONOMY 6:1–9

Our oldest daughter, Lisa, was preparing to get married, and I found myself doing things I don't normally do. I paid for stuff I wouldn't otherwise buy. I grew interested in things I don't care much about: decorations, catering, candles.

And I reflected. As I thought back on the twenty-two years that had gone into the preparation for the big day, a couple of things stood out.

The first was the wonder of it all. Just the other day (it seems) my little girl had ringlets in her hair as a preschool mascot for the basketball team I coached. Now she was a high school music teacher about to become the wife of a youth pastor.

The second thing that stood out was the thrill of knowing she had made it this far by God's instruction. She had learned what it is "to be taught by the Lord," as Isaiah put it (54:13). Only God could have touched her heart to receive salvation. Only the Holy Spirit could direct her in the right paths. Only God's teaching is flawless.

No matter how much we strive to prepare our children for life, none of it matters without "the training and instruction of the Lord" (Ephesians 6:4). Whether we're preparing them for kindergarten or for a wedding, that's the basis for training that will last a lifetime.   —DAVE BRANON

Watch Your Mouth

From the fruit of his lips a man is filled with good things
*   as surely as the work of his hands rewards him.*
The way of a fool seems right to him,
*   but a wise man listens to advice.*
A fool shows his annoyance at once,
*   but a prudent man overlooks an insult.*
A truthful witness gives honest testimony,
*   but a false witness tells lies.*
Reckless words pierce like a sword,
*   but the tongue of the wise brings healing.*
Truthful lips endure forever,
*   but a lying tongue lasts only a moment.*
There is deceit in the hearts of those who plot evil,
*   but joy for those who promote peace.*
No harm befalls the righteous,
*   but the wicked have their fill of trouble.*
The LORD *detests lying lips,*
*   but he delights in men who are truthful.*
A prudent man keeps his knowledge to himself,
*   but the heart of fools blurts out folly.*
Diligent hands will rule,
*   but laziness ends in slave labor.*
An anxious heart weighs a man down,
*   but a kind word cheers him up.* —PROVERBS 12:14–25

*Y*ou have probably heard the childish taunt, "Sticks and stones may break my bones, but words can never hurt me." This piece of folk wisdom is at best a half-truth, with the second half being totally untrue. While sticks and stones can bring instant injury and pain, words can produce even worse and longer-lasting hurt.

According to a news report, an eight-year-old was arrested for assaulting a playmate with a stick. But the damage got worse when the parents waged a war of words that carried the humiliation and embarrassment of the children into the national press.

Sticks and stones inflict wounds that usually heal in time. But words can go much deeper and cause pain that lasts a lifetime. Such words as "I don't love you," "You are a failure," and "You're no good" can do permanent damage. Some people have been so deeply wounded that they are unable to accept words such as "I love you," "You're special," and "I appreciate you."

The book of Proverbs urges us to watch our words (12:17–22; 15:4; 26:2). We ought to pray with the psalmist, "May the words of my mouth and the meditation of my heart be pleasing in your sight, O LORD, my Rock and my redeemer" (Psalm 19:14).
                                                              —MART DE HAAN

Name upon Name

A record of the genealogy of Jesus Christ the son of David, the son of Abraham:

> Abraham was the father of Isaac,
> Isaac the father of Jacob,
> Jacob the father of Judah and his brothers,
> Judah the father of Perez and Zerah, whose mother was Tamar,
> Perez the father of Hezron,
> Hezron the father of Ram,
> Ram the father of Amminadab,
> Amminadab the father of Nahshon,
> Nahshon the father of Salmon,
> Salmon the father of Boaz, whose mother was Rahab,
> Boaz the father of Obed, whose mother was Ruth,
> Obed the father of Jesse,
> and Jesse the father of King David.
> David was the father of Solomon, whose mother had been Uriah's wife, . . .
> and . . . Joseph, the husband of Mary, of whom was born Jesus, who is called Christ.

Thus there were fourteen generations in all from Abraham to David, fourteen from David to the exile to Babylon, and fourteen from the exile to the Christ.   —MATTHEW 1:1–6, 16–17

*D*alton Conley, a sociologist at New York University, and his wife, Natalie Jeremijenko, have two children. Several years ago, they sought permission from the city to change their five-year-old son's name to Yo Xing Heyno Augustus Eisner Alexander Weiser Knuckles Jeremijenko-Conley. Actually, a lot of that name was already his, but his parents added three of the middle names. They had specific reasons for each one.

I believe that God had specific reasons for the names He included in the beginning of Matthew's gospel. It may seem like a long, boring list of meaningless names, but those names served at least two purposes. First, they provided the framework by which true Hebrews could establish their family roots and maintain religious purity against outside influences. Second, the names reflected the sovereign work of God. They revealed God's dealings in the past, which resulted in the birth of the Messiah. The Lord used all kinds of people in Jesus' lineage—farmers, kings, a prostitute, adulterers, liars. When we read this list, we are reminded of God's faithfulness.

As you think about being a part of God's family by faith in Christ, remember His faithfulness to you and His desire to use you to bring about His purposes.　　—MARVIN WILLIAMS

The Other Side of Thank You

If I speak in the tongues of men and of angels, but have not love, I am only a resounding gong or a clanging cymbal. If I have the gift of prophecy and can fathom all mysteries and all knowledge, and if I have a faith that can move mountains, but have not love, I am nothing. If I give all I possess to the poor and surrender my body to the flames, but have not love, I gain nothing.

Love is patient, love is kind. It does not envy, it does not boast, it is not proud. It is not rude, it is not self-seeking, it is not easily angered, it keeps no record of wrongs. Love does not delight in evil but rejoices with the truth. It always protects, always trusts, always hopes, always perseveres.

Love never fails. But where there are prophecies, they will cease; where there are tongues, they will be stilled; where there is knowledge, it will pass away. For we know in part and we prophesy in part, but when perfection comes, the imperfect disappears . . . . Now we see but a poor reflection as in a mirror; then we shall see face to face. Now I know in part; then I shall know fully, even as I am fully known.

And now these three remain: faith, hope and love. But the greatest of these is love. —1 Corinthians 13:1–10, 12–13

A baby gift came to a young couple who were new parents. They were grateful for the present, so the mom picked up a thank-you card, wrote a nice note, and got it ready to send.

Somehow it got buried in an avalanche of paperwork and was never mailed—and the thank-you was forgotten. The gift-givers waited, but no acknowledgment came.

A rift developed as one family thought the thank-you had been given, while the other thought the lack of a thank-you was a snub. This inadvertent failure to send a card left the gift-giver feeling slighted, unappreciated, and neglected.

Among the most important words we can speak are the two words, "Thank you." And while it is vital to be grateful, there's another side of thank you. If we bestow a gift on another, we should do so out of a motive that doesn't expect anything, even a thank-you, in return. True love gives with no expectations.

Love, as described in 1 Corinthians 13:4, is patient and kind, and is never self-seeking. Love keeps no record of wrongs— even if someone forgets to thank us for a kindness. The other side of thank you is a pure heart that reflects God's perfect love for us.   —DAVE BRANON

Change Your Name

One day Peter and John were going up to the temple at the time of prayer—at three in the afternoon. Now a man crippled from birth was being carried to the temple gate called Beautiful, where he was put every day to beg from those going into the temple courts. When he saw Peter and John about to enter, he asked them for money. Peter looked straight at him, as did John. Then Peter said, "Look at us!" So the man gave them his attention, expecting to get something from them.

Then Peter said, "Silver or gold I do not have, but what I have I give you. In the name of Jesus Christ of Nazareth, walk." Taking him by the right hand, he helped him up, and instantly the man's feet and ankles became strong. He jumped to his feet and began to walk. Then he went with them into the temple courts, walking and jumping, and praising God. When all the people saw him walking and praising God, they recognized him as the same man who used to sit begging at the temple gate called Beautiful, and they were filled with wonder and amazement at what had happened to him.

—ACTS 3:1–10

*N*ames are important. Parents may spend months researching and deciding on the perfect name for their baby. Often the final decision is based on its sound, uniqueness, or meaning.

One woman took on a new name because she disliked her original name. She mistakenly believed that changing it could alter her destiny. That's not likely, but for those who trust in Jesus as their Savior and are from that time on identified by His name, a radical transformation does take place.

There is a powerful significance attached to the name of Jesus. The apostles performed miracles (Acts 3:6–7, 16; 4:10) and cast out demons in His name (Luke 10:17). They spoke and taught in the name of Jesus. They baptized believers in the name of Jesus (Acts 2:38). And it is only through the name of Jesus that we gain access to the Father (Acts 4:12).

When we become Christians, we share in that worthy name. And as we follow Christ, we are able to reflect His light to any darkness we encounter, whether in our neighborhood, our workplace, or even our home. Our prayer should be that when people see us—they will see Christ.

Our names may have meaning or significance. But to bear the name Christian is life-transforming.   —CINDY KASPER

Mirror Image

Now if the ministry that brought death, which was engraved in letters on stone, came with glory, so that the Israelites could not look steadily at the face of Moses because of its glory, fading though it was, will not the ministry of the Spirit be even more glorious? If the ministry that condemns men is glorious, how much more glorious is the ministry that brings righteousness! For what was glorious has no glory now in comparison with the surpassing glory. And if what was fading away came with glory, how much greater is the glory of that which lasts!

Therefore, since we have such a hope, we are very bold. We are not like Moses, who would put a veil over his face to keep the Israelites from gazing at it while the radiance was fading away. But their minds were made dull, for to this day the same veil remains when the old covenant is read. It has not been removed, because only in Christ is it taken away. Even to this day when Moses is read, a veil covers their hearts. But whenever anyone turns to the Lord, the veil is taken away. Now the Lord is the Spirit, and where the Spirit of the Lord is, there is freedom. And we, who with unveiled faces all reflect the Lord's glory, are being transformed into his likeness with ever-increasing glory, which comes from the Lord, who is the Spirit.

—2 Corinthians 3:7–18

*Y*ears ago, an elderly businessman asked me, "What is your biggest problem?"

I pondered this for a while before replying: "When I look in the mirror every morning, I see my biggest problem staring at me."

Today's Scripture reading teaches me that Christians are to be like mirrors. Paul said that our faces are not to be veiled. This is logical. No one installs a mirror and then places a curtain over it. A covered mirror will not fulfill the purpose of reflecting the objects before it.

In 2 Corinthians 3:18, we are described as "beholding as in a mirror the glory of the Lord" (NKJV). When we behold His glory, we will be "transformed into the same image"—that is, the likeness of Christ.

We may wonder why we are still so far from being like Christ in our thinking and behavior. Perhaps this question will help: "Whose life do we mirror?"

God's people must reflect God's glory. To do that we must make it our habit to behold His glory. We must read and meditate on His Word. We must pray and trust God's Holy Spirit to work in our hearts. Only then can we obey His commands and depend on His promises.

Whose glory are you reflecting today?   —ALBERT LEE

Walking in His Dust

As Jesus walked beside the Sea of Galilee, he saw Simon and his brother Andrew casting a net into the lake, for they were fishermen. "Come, follow me," Jesus said, "and I will make you fishers of men." At once they left their nets and followed him.

When he had gone a little farther, he saw James son of Zebedee and his brother John in a boat, preparing their nets. Without delay he called them, and they left their father Zebedee in the boat with the hired men and followed him. —MARK 1:16–20

*I*n the first century, a Jewish man who wanted to become a disciple of a rabbi (teacher) was expected to leave family and job to join his rabbi. They would live together twenty-four hours a day—walking from place to place, teaching and learning, studying and working. They discussed and memorized the Scriptures and applied them to life.

The disciple's calling, as described in early Jewish writings about basic ethics, was to "cover himself in the dust of [the rabbi's] feet," drinking in his every word. He followed his rabbi so closely that he would "walk in his dust." In doing so, he became like the rabbi, his master.

Simon, Andrew, James, and John knew that this was the type of relationship to which Jesus was calling them (Mark 1:16–20). So immediately they walked away from their work and "went after Him" (v. 20). For three years they stayed close to Him—listening to His teaching, watching His miracles, learning His principles, and walking in His dust.

As Jesus' followers today, we too can "walk in His dust." By spending time studying and meditating on His Word and applying its principles to life, we'll become like our rabbi—Jesus.

—ANNE CETAS

About the Authors

Henry Bosch served as the first editor of the daily devotional booklet that became *Our Daily Bread* (ODB) and contributed many of the earliest articles. He was also one of the singers on the Radio Bible Class live broadcast.

Dave Branon has done freelance writing for many years and has published more than thirteen books. Dave taught English and coached basketball and baseball at the high school level before coming to RBC Ministries (RBC), where he is now the Managing Editor of *Sports Spectrum* magazine.

Anne Cetas is Assistant Managing Editor on the editorial staff at RBC Ministries and has been with the ministry for twenty-five years. Anne and her husband, Carl, also work as mentors in an inner-city ministry. "It's the most challenging ministry I've ever loved," says Anne. She also teaches Sunday school and disciples new believers.

Bill Crowder spent over twenty years in pastoral ministry and is now Director of Church Ministries and Director of Publications for RBC Ministries. Bill is the author of *The Spotlight of Faith, The Path of His Passion,* and *Overcoming Life's Challenges.*

Dennis De Haan is a nephew of RBC founder Dr. M. R. De Haan. He pastored two churches in Iowa and Michigan before joining the RBC staff in 1971. He served as the Associate Editor of ODB from 1973 until 1982 and then as Editor until June 1995. Now retired, Dennis continues editing for ODB on a part-time basis.

Mart De Haan is the grandson of RBC founder Dr. M. R. De Haan, and the son of former president, Richard W. De Haan. Mart is the president of RBC Ministries and is heard regularly on the *Discover the Word* radio program and seen on *Day of Discovery* television. Mart is also a contributing writer for ODB, the Discovery Series Bible study booklets, and a monthly column on timely issues called "Been Thinking About."

Dr. M. R. De Haan was the founder of Radio Bible Class and one of the founders of *Our Daily Bread*. A physician who later in life became a pastor, he was well known for his gravelly voice and impassioned Bible teaching. His commitment to ministry was to lead people of all nations to personal faith and maturity in Christ. The Grand Rapids, Michigan-based RBC Ministries continues to build upon the spiritual foundation of Dr. De Haan's vision and work.

Richard De Haan was President of RBC Ministries and teacher on RBC programs for twenty years. He was the son of RBC founder Dr. M. R. De Haan and wrote a number of full-length books and study booklets for RBC. Often called "the encourager," Richard was committed to faithfulness to God's Word and to integrity as a ministry. Richard went to be with the Lord in 2002.

Dave Egner is now retired from RBC. He was (until June 2002) Managing Editor of *Campus Journal*. He has written Discovery Series study booklets and articles for a variety of publications. Dave taught English and writing for ten years at Grand Rapids Baptist College (now Cornerstone University) before coming to RBC.

Dennis Fisher joined RBC Ministries in 1998, and since 2005 he has been infusing *Our Daily Bread* with illustrations from history, literature, and science. As a young adult, Dennis felt the need to be trained in God's Word, and his thirst for the Word led him to Bible college and seminary. After serving on campus ministries and with church pastoral staff for ten years, he became the professor of Evangelism and Discipleship at Moody Bible Institute for eight years. "*Our Daily Bread* was an encouragement to me during a time of trial and now it is a privilege to write for the devotional," says Dennis.

Vernon Grounds, Chancellor of Denver Seminary, has had an extensive preaching, teaching, and counseling ministry and was president of Denver Seminary. In addition to writing articles for ODB, he has also written many books and magazine articles.

Cindy Kasper has served at RBC for more than thirty years, most recently as Associate Editor for *Our Journey.* She's an experienced author, having written youth devotional articles for more than a decade.

Albert Lee is the Director of International Ministries for RBC and has the passion, vision, and energy to help RBC Ministries spread its work. He grew up in Singapore, attended Singapore Bible College and Taylor University in Indiana, and served with youth for Christ from 1971 to 1999.

Julie Ackerman Link is a seasoned writer and editor who has worked on many projects for RBC Ministries and Discovery House Publishers, including the Loving God series. She has been writing for *Our Daily Bread* since December 2000.

David McCasland researches and helps develop biographical documentaries for *Day of Discovery* television, in addition to writing ODB articles. His books include the award-winning biography *Oswald Chambers: Abandoned to God*, a compilation of *The Complete Works of Oswald Chambers*, and *Pure Gold*, a biography of Eric Liddell.

Joe Stowell serves as teaching pastor at Harvest Bible Chapel in suburban Chicago. He served for eighteen years as president of Moody Bible Institute, and he now partners with RBC Ministries in radio, writing, and television productions. He has written many books, including *Radical Reliance, Eternity,* and *The Upside of Down.*

Paul Van Gorder began writing regularly for ODB in 1969 and continued until 1992. He also served as associate Bible teacher for the *Day of Discovery* television program and traveled extensively as a speaker for Radio Bible Class. He and his wife now live in retirement in South Carolina.

Herb Vander Lugt remained a vital contributor to *Our Daily Bread* up to the time he went to be with his Lord and Savior on December 2, 2006. He served as Senior Research Editor for RBC Ministries and had been with the ministry since 1966, when he became the third author to contribute to *Our Daily Bread*. In addition to his devotional articles, he wrote numerous Discovery Series booklets and reviewed all study and devotional materials. Herb pastored six churches and held three interim ministerial positions after retiring from the pastorate in 1989.

Marvin Williams is one of the lead pastors at Tabernacle Comnuity Church in Grand Rapids, Michigan. Educated at Biship College in Dallas, Texas, and Trinity Evangelical Divinity School in Deerfield, Illinois, he has also been associate pastor of youth at New Hope Baptist Church and assistant pastor at Calvary Church, both in Grand Rapids. Marvin frequently refers to the guiding principle found in Joshua 1:8, "This Book of the Law shall not depart from your mouth, but you shall meditate in it day and night, that you may observe to do according to all that is written in it."

Joanie Yoder, a favorite among ODB readers, went home to be with her Savior in 2004. She and her husband established a Christian rehabilitation center for drug addicts in England many years ago. Widowed in 1982, she wrote with hope about true dependence on God and his life-changing power.